# Anytime Coaching
## Unleashing Employee Performance
## Second Edition

# Anytime Coaching
## Unleashing Employee Performance
## Second Edition

Teresa Wedding Kloster
Wendy Sherwin Swire

MANAGEMENTCONCEPTSPRESS

**MANAGEMENT**CONCEPTS PRESS

8230 Leesburg Pike, Suite 800
Tysons Corner, VA 22182
(703) 790-9595
Fax: (703) 790-1371
www.managementconcepts.com

Printed in the United States of America

Library of Congress Control Number: 2014954261

ISBN 978-1-56726-480-7

eISBN 978-1-56726-481-4

## Praise for *Anytime Coaching: Unleashing Employee Performance, Second Edition*

*"Expanded and updated with the latest research from the fields of neuroscience and mindfulness, this new edition of* Anytime Coaching *is a well-organized, easy-to-read roadmap for managers and leaders who want to unlock the potential of their team members through coaching. Once you read it, you'll use it again and again as an essential reference on your leadership bookshelf."*

—SCOTT EBLIN, AUTHOR, *THE NEXT LEVEL* AND *OVERWORKED AND OVERWHELMED*

*"*Anytime Coaching *is absolutely one of the most practical guides to effective coaching I have encountered in my 20 years as a certified coach. Cover-to-cover, the book is full of valuable tools. The integration of new findings from neuroscience and mindfulness helps leaders and coaches deepen their understanding not only of the 'what' and the 'how,' but also the 'why,' of effective coaching. Enthusiastically recommended for beginning and experienced coaches and managers alike. Well, well done!"*

—CHALMERS BROTHERS, AUTHOR, *LANGUAGE AND THE PURSUIT OF HAPPINESS*

*"*Anytime Coaching *provides a very useful blueprint for building a 'coaching culture' in any type of organization—large or small, private or government, profit or nonprofit—by focusing on the four most important underlying coaching skills. With its addition of the latest insights from the fields of neuroscience and mindfulness, I highly recommend* Anytime Coaching *for anyone seeking to make their organization a more humane and productive place to work."*

—ED MODELL, JD, PCC, PAST PRESIDENT, INTERNATIONAL COACH FEDERATION

*"So much of being a leader is about knowing yourself, being present, and being ready to handle whatever comes your way. Teresa and Wendy, leaders in the executive coaching field, bring science, experience, and strategic thinking, together with practical recommendations, to handle just about any situation. Anytime Coaching enables readers to hone the leadership skills necessary to advance at any level."*

—Brook Colangelo, EVP and Chief Technology Officer,
Houghton Mifflin Harcourt
Former CIO of the Executive Office of the President and White House

*"The second edition is even more powerful than the original! It continues the original edition's pragmatic and grounded approach to accelerating learning and growth in others. Losing nothing from the original edition, this one enlivens the content and increases its impact by skillfully weaving in recent breakthroughs in the fields of neuroscience and mindfulness in a way that is accessible and actionable. It has my strongest recommendation."*

—Frank Ball, MCC, Faculty Member
Institute for Transformational Leadership, Georgetown University

*"Anytime Coaching is a leader's go-to resource for achieving true individual and organizational success. I have underlined many sections to share with my team, family, and friends. Anytime Coaching keeps me grounded and focused at work and home; these models have helped me lead a better life professionally and personally."*

—Laura Fuentes, Senior Vice President, Human Resources,
Hilton International

"Kloster and Swire's simple, elegant model will enable you to turn 'coachable moments' into powerful breakthroughs. Use this book if you are a leader who wants to motivate your employees, an executive coach working to help your clients achieve their goals, or even if you're new to coaching. Put this book at the top of your coaching books—it has it all!"

—DR. CYNTHIA ROMAN, PCC, COAUTHOR, ORGANIZATIONAL COACHING
RETIRED ASSOCIATE PROFESSOR OF MANAGEMENT, MARYMOUNT UNIVERSITY

"The book provides insightful knowledge and practical tools that enable managers and policymakers to become better at listening, asking, and empowering others to achieve greater results. Thank you, Teresa and Wendy, for reminding us once again that in order to move faster, we first need to slow down and listen."

—LOURDES MELGAR DE LOPEZ PRESA, PhD
MEXICO'S DEPUTY SECRETARY OF ENERGY FOR HYDROCARBONS

"Whether you're a first-time supervisor eager to build the foundational skills to ensure your effectiveness in the role, or a seasoned manager looking for ways to take your game to the next level, Anytime Coaching is your answer. Filled with straightforward and clear guidance on the skills and approaches necessary for effectively managing in today's challenging work environments, this book couldn't be more essential."

—STEVE HELLER
PROGRAM DIRECTOR, LEADERSHIP COACHING CERTIFICATE PROGRAM
INSTITUTE FOR TRANSFORMATIONAL LEADERSHIP, GEORGETOWN UNIVERSITY

"This book, with its thoughtful and deliberate approach to leadership development, is a must read for anyone interested in growing as a leader. It provides valuable tools and actionable guidance that transform important concepts into real solutions."

—DOUG MORAN
AUTHOR, IF YOU WILL LEAD: ENDURING WISDOM FOR 21ST CENTURY LEADERS

*"Few leadership qualities have surfaced in the past several years as important as the ability to enhance performance and drive business results through coaching. Whether you work internally to an organization or as an external coach/consultant, Anytime Coaching is a practical guide to improving performance. I recommend it to anyone who is serious about improving their coaching skills."*

—MARSHA KING, PHD, ADJUNCT PROFESSOR, NORTHWESTERN UNIVERSITY
PRESIDENT, SKILLPOINT CONSULTING, INC.

*"As a relatively new manager, I have been searching for resources that contain tips for communicating and leading. I especially enjoyed the discussions about the practices of inquiring and extreme listening and have already seen the benefits of putting what I learned into action."*

—MELISSA FEUER, JD, EXECUTIVE DIRECTOR
OFFICE FOR STUDENT ENGAGEMENT, GEORGE WASHINGTON
UNIVERSITY'S COLLEGE OF PROFESSIONAL STUDIES

*"Kloster and Swire's new edition is a useful and practical guide for busy managers who want to integrate some of the new neuroscience and mindfulness findings into their performance coaching of their people. The tools and approaches form a helpful guide to the sometimes elusive territory of holding real coaching conversations."*

—DOUG SILSBEE, AUTHOR, *PRESENCE-BASED COACHING*

*"This book is an exceptional guide for how to become an impactful and empowered manager and leader of others. This new edition's focus on neuroscience and mindfulness connects managers and leaders to the most essential element of success— emotional intelligence—and shows them how to grow and use it."*

—LAVERNE WEBB, CO-FOUNDER AND CEO, ENCOMPASS LLC

"Anytime Coaching *is a thought-provoking and easy-to-follow practical guide to improving one's management style, written in a way that compels the reader to practice its principles. As a government manager with over 25 years' experience managing diverse teams, I wish I had had such a guide available years ago.*"
—RICHARD M. WILBUR, RETIRED LIEUTENANT COMMANDER, US NAVY
FORMER STATE DEPARTMENT FOREIGN SERVICE OFFICER

"*Part common sense, part higher level thinking, part introspection,* Anytime Coaching *is a must read for anyone, whether in a managerial position or working on the front lines. It's a wonderful book about developing healthy practices, not only on the job but in our day-to-day lives. I endorse this book without reservation.*"
—DR. STEPHEN M. HELLMAN, M.D.

"*At a time when leaders at all levels are expected to coach, this new edition of a classic work provides a simple yet powerful framework for bringing out the best in people. The tools and techniques these masterful coaches share can work with anyone, anywhere, anytime.*"
—CAROL GOLDSMITH, PCC, NLPT
PAST PRESIDENT, INTERNATIONAL COACH FEDERATION
METRO DC CHARTER CHAPTER

"*Every day I face a myriad of decisions, each of varying complexity and priority. The framework of* Anytime Coaching *provides me with a clear methodology to integrate into my interactions in the workplace to achieve focus and results. The approach is set out in clear and practical terms to ensure results.*"
—JONATHAN GORDON, CHIEF FINANCIAL OFFICER
WELLESLEY INFORMATION SERVICES

# About the Authors

**Teresa Wedding Kloster** is an executive coach and consultant in leadership development. With over 15 years of leadership and management experience in a corporate setting, she supports client organizations by designing leadership development strategies and programs, by coaching leaders at all levels, and through delivering workshops on a wide variety of topics, including leadership, management and coaching skills, emotional intelligence, critical thinking, and performance management. Her company, Kloster & Associates, serves clients in both the private and public sectors, in the United States and abroad.

Ms. Kloster has a certificate in Leadership Coaching from Georgetown University and also holds an International Coach Federation credential. She earned a Master of Arts in Education and a Bachelor of Arts in English Literature from the College of William and Mary. She is a member of the International Coach Federation.

**Wendy Sherwin Swire** is Principal of Swire Solutions, LLC, a consulting firm that improves workplace performance through executive coaching, consulting, training, neuroleadership, and conflict resolution services. She delivers courses on executive coaching, management, neuroleadership, conflict resolution, influencing, and communication in both the private and public sectors. Ms. Swire has worked with clients throughout the United States as well as in Asia, Europe, Latin America, and Africa. Prior to forming Swire Solutions, she was an international economist for the federal government and worked in the financial services industry.

Ms. Swire served as an Adjunct Professor at the Carey Graduate School of Business at Johns Hopkins University. She graduated from Georgetown University's Leadership Coaching Program and holds a Professional Certified Coach credential from the International Coach Federation. She received a Master's Degree from Tufts University's Fletcher School of Law and Diplomacy and a Bachelor of Arts in International Relations and Economics from Mount Holyoke College. Ms. Swire runs the DC Neuroleadership Group. She is a member of the International Coach Federation, the Society for Neuroscience, and the Conflict Resolution Center of Montgomery County.

To the many leaders everywhere who earnestly want
to make a positive difference in the lives of those with
whom they work. And to the many leaders, managers, and
teachers whose patient and kind coaching conversations
with me continue to make a lasting difference.

—TWK

Once again, to Andy, Sam, and Mattie, who provide me
with my source of love and meaning not just anytime, but
all the time.

—WSS

# Contents

# Preface
## Anytime Coaching Revisited

Since the 2009 publication of *Anytime Coaching: Unleashing Employee Performance*, we have had conversations with numerous leaders who read and applied its principles. Many found the book instrumental in helping them in everyday conversations—as team members, non-supervisors, volunteers working in their communities, even parents. Our readers have enthusiastically shared their stories of how Anytime Coaching helped them in the following ways:

- Becoming more aware of the "self" they bring to their workplace
- Slowing down to observe themselves and those around them more consciously
- Hearing their employees' ideas and concerns more empathetically
- Developing richer work relationships
- Asking more insightful questions
- Having more productive difficult conversations

■ Being more deliberate when responding to others

■ Continuing along the path to greater expertise in being an Anytime Coach.

We learned from these conversations that whether dealing with the realities and the aftereffects of an economic recession, navigating intergenerational relationships in the workplace, or keeping up with the pace of change in the workplace, the principles of Anytime Coaching are truly helping people achieve greater fulfillment and success at work.

Something else of huge importance has been happening since the original publication. The intersecting disciplines of neuroscience and mindfulness have been uncovering more data about the individual's ability to build resilience through specific practices that train the brain. Yes, "train the brain." This development has led us to refocus the four Anytime Coaching practices to encompass the newest wisdom of both neuroscience and mindfulness.

Neuroscience comprises the scientific disciplines that explore the structure and workings of the brain and nervous system. In this revised edition, we focus on the truly amazing "bossy" brain, which not only controls your body and how you move but also what you think, feel, remember, and learn—whether you are aware of its control or not. Using technologies that allow more precision while observing the brain, neuroscientists can now describe the brain's workings in greater detail and verify how the brain can be "rewired" for greater effectiveness, creativity, empathy, and happiness. In this updated edition, we share how recent discoveries in neuroscience support the practices of Anytime Coaching.

In the context of Anytime Coaching, we use the term "mindfulness" to mean regularly and deliberately stilling the mind as a way to develop the day-to-day capability of being fully attentive and aware in the moment. In the last decade, we have witnessed greater interest and new research on the intersection of neuroscience and mindfulness—how mental activity can strengthen control over the brain's workings. The research offers positive news: Mindfulness increases attention, enhances cognitive performance, and has other healthy side effects. We interviewed mindfulness experts and have included new exercises that make mindfulness accessible to our readers.

Each chapter in this second edition retains the central principles presented in the original publication. Additions include applicable information describing how data from the field of neuroscience and the discipline of mindfulness support, enhance, expand, or underscore those principles. We are excited to share insights from these two disciplines with our readers.

## Why Anytime Coaching?

As professional coaches, we have had the privilege of helping hundreds of clients become more effective leaders, managers, and contributors in a variety of organizations. These clients work in the federal government, private industry, entrepreneurial businesses, and nonprofit organizations. Many of our clients became interested in coaching and asked us to share the models and techniques for how we approach our work. We noticed that as our clients incorporated coaching practices into their daily work, they started to get better and better performance from their employees.

As part of our research, we interviewed managers and leaders who shared with us their experiences coaching their employees. These interviews confirmed what we suspected: Managers are hungry for more practical tools and information not only for themselves but also for their employees. We also know from firsthand experience that coaching becomes a way of life—a way of being. As coaches, we constantly look for opportunities to bring out the best in people, to help them raise the bar on their work and life. We ask questions and listen intently to discover new, positive possibilities. We observe and reframe to help people shift their perspectives and create new solutions. We respond with clarity to what we hear. For us, coaching is part of our way of interacting with others at work—anytime. So Anytime Coaching was born.

In putting together a practical guide to Anytime Coaching, we sought to make the skills and principles accessible to anyone interested in improving the quality and results of interactions with employees. We wanted the tips and techniques to be simple enough that managers could learn them quickly and use them every day in their interactions with employees.

In this new edition, we have added stories from readers and clients that illustrate how an Anytime Coaching practice played out in the real world. For these stories, we are grateful to the generosity of our readers and clients who described their successes using Anytime Coaching principles in their work lives.

## Who Can Use Anytime Coaching?

Anyone who has conversations with other people, both within and outside the workplace, can benefit from the core principles of Anytime Coaching. At the office, whether you lead a temporary, cross-functional team on a short-term project or formally manage large groups of people on a daily basis, you can use Anytime Coaching to achieve better results. In today's fast-moving and rapidly changing workplace, more and more employees find themselves relying on others to get work done without the title and authority to demand cooperation. They too can use Anytime Coaching as:

- The pathway to individual and organizational performance
- A way of working with people that focuses on positive possibilities
- A set of flexible and adaptable practices that builds on every-day behaviors
- A set of skills that helps them develop others while getting work done.

When you are engaged in Anytime Coaching, you are:

- Partnering with others to jointly create desired outcomes
- Creating alliances with your employees, coworkers, and boss to seek solutions that support the organization's mission
- Helping people solve issues with their own best thinking
- Seeing every interaction with an employee as a chance to help him or her shine
- Being a manager who helps your employees grow
- Improving employee performance.

## The Anytime Coaching Model

We present the key practices of Anytime Coaching in a simple model that anyone can understand and apply immediately. Our intent is to supplement the body of work on coaching with a practical guide that is designed to be especially helpful to the front-line managers in today's rapidly changing workplace. We hope that managers ranging from the first-time supervisor to the most senior executive will find practical coaching tools they can use immediately to transform the way they work with employees and colleagues. In addition, we have interwoven findings from the worlds of neuroscience and mindfulness, describing how those findings help illuminate the more practical aspects of Anytime Coaching.

## ■ ■ ■ How This Book Is Organized

This book begins and ends with chapters focused on the anytime coach's own self. The intervening chapters focus on the four practices of Anytime Coaching and the performance improvements they help create.

**Chapter 1, It All Begins with You,** emphasizes the importance of both self-awareness and organizational awareness. Before you begin learning Anytime Coaching practices, it is important to assess your own thinking about work, your role as a manager, and the organization in which you work and achieve results. The chapter includes exercises designed to help you increase your awareness of the self you bring to Anytime Coaching.

**Chapter 2, The Practice of Observing,** helps you see with new eyes. You will learn how to view your employees and the work you do in fresh and positive ways. This chapter focuses on nonverbal cues and emotions. In this updated edition, you will also discover how the practice of mindfulness can enhance your ability to observe yourself and others. Some practical tools and exercises to help you be more present, aware, and focused in day-to-day interactions are included.

**Chapter 3, The Practice of Inquiring,** expands your ability to ask insightful and powerful questions when coaching your employees. You will learn to distinguish among types of questions and their uses.

**Chapter 4, The Practice of Listening,** will guide you toward becoming an extreme listener. This chapter builds on the practices of observing and inquiring to leverage your ability to listen deeply and truly understand what others are saying.

**Chapter 5, The Practice of Responding,** focuses on how to respond once you have observed, inquired, and listened. You will learn about responding with clear intention, using tools that will help you consciously and purposefully create powerful coaching conversations.

**Chapter 6, Improving Day-to-Day Performance,** shows how applying the practices of Anytime Coaching triggers small shifts in day-to-day performance and explores how those shifts yield improved individual and organizational performance over time. You will learn how to sustain the focus on performance, how to refocus when coaching conversations get off track, and how to share feedback.

**Chapter 7, Your Path to Becoming an Anytime Coach,** focuses on your continuous learning and development as an anytime coach. It provides guidelines for planning your development as an anytime coach as well as tips and techniques for honing your skills.

To assist you on the path to becoming an effective anytime coach, the book includes the following elements:

- *Anytime Coaching model.* The model comprises four interrelated practices (observing, inquiring, listening, and responding), supported by self-awareness, self-development, mindfulness, and neuroscience. At the center of the model is what happens when anytime coaches apply the practices in combination: improved day-to-day performance.
- *Principles.* Short, highlighted statements throughout the text convey key messages about Anytime Coaching.
- *Exercises.* These opportunities to explore, reflect on, and practice key concepts and techniques include self-assessments and self-reflective questions.
- *Practice tools.* These tools and techniques will help you practice and apply the Anytime Coaching approach.
- *Stories.* Real-world examples of coaching situations illustrate specific practices and techniques.

■ *Website.* The Anytime Coaching website includes exclusive coaching resources and tools designed to help you put Anytime Coaching practices to work. To access the website, please visit *www.ManagementConcepts.com/AnytimeCoaching* and enter the user name FutureCoach and the password MCP2015.

We have walked in your shoes. We understand the energy and performance that can be unleashed when employees know they are honored and respected. Coaching, at its most fundamental level, honors and respects everyone in working relationships. You will discover how this is accomplished as you work toward becoming an anytime coach.

We have witnessed the many positive results of coaching. Our hope is that you will find immediate use for the practices in this book, and that this book will be one you consult often as you would a knowledgeable friend.

*Teresa Wedding Kloster*
*Wendy Sherwin Swire*
Washington, D.C.

# Acknowledgments

We once again extend our deep gratitude to the numerous leaders, managers, and executives who shared with us the many ways they used the techniques presented in the first edition of *Anytime Coaching* in their day-to-day work. We learned firsthand how these managers and leaders applied Anytime Coaching practices and heard personal accounts of their successes and challenges leading in today's workplace. We interviewed managers in federal government agencies, Fortune 100 leaders, new managers, and seasoned executives. We were gratified to hear how the first edition of our book made a difference in their workplaces. Thank you to the leaders and managers we cited in the book and the many others who helped shape this new edition. We also thank our clients for the privilege of serving as their coaches and for never failing to teach us valuable lessons about coaching even as we assist them.

We continue to proudly acknowledge the faculty of the Georgetown University Leadership Coaching Program and the Institute for Transformational Leadership for improving our understanding of the art of coaching and for coaching us to even greater competency. Our colleagues and friends from the Georgetown coaching community served as a source of support and encouragement throughout our training as well as in writing both editions and beyond.

We remain indebted to the wonderful publishing team at Management Concepts, who asked and encouraged us to write the second edition, especially Myra Strauss, who was unendingly cheerful and helpful every step of the way.

For the new application and content on neuroscience and mindfulness found in this second edition, we owe special gratitude to the longstanding members of the DC Neuroleadership Group (and former DC Neuroleadership LIG), who help make learning neuroscience a joy, Dr. M.A. Greenstein of the Greenstein Institute for her support, and the many mindfulness teachers whose patience and wisdom continue to increase ours.

Kathy Johnson at Management Concepts deserves special thanks. Kathy encouraged us to revisit and update the first edition, provided thoughtful feedback throughout the process, and continues to have a strong vision to support coaching that is accessible to many different leadership audiences. Thanks to Allison Tardif for her help with graphic design and support and Anna Mauldin for her expertise as well as for going the extra mile to spread the word about Anytime Coaching.

We are especially grateful to our families and friends, who once again patiently supported us throughout the entire project. Wendy would like to acknowledge her husband, Andy, for his thoughtfulness and support.

Writing is a solitary endeavor. Finally, we acknowledge the value of working as co-authors. We believe that having another respected colleague constantly available to validate, question, and enhance our work has made the second edition of *Anytime Coaching: Unleashing Employee Performance* more enjoyable to create and more valuable to you, the reader.

# INTRODUCTION
## Anytime Coaching in a Changing World

The workplace is ever-changing: the economic pressures of recession and recovery; the increasing exodus of seasoned leaders; the influx of a technologically savvy generation with new ways of working; greater acceptance of flexible hours and where work gets done; pressure to focus on many priorities at once; and the constant focus on results. All these realities have combined to make today's workplace both an exciting and a challenging place to be a manager.

Methods of managing and supervising employees are also changing, and in fact, must change. Managers are finding that coaching skills are the keys that enable both employees and their leaders to get results in today's redefined work environment. There is a growing realization that the command-and-control practices of the past are not as effective with today's employees and may even be counterproductive. Today's most successful leaders know that coaching is a vital set of skills to be used *anytime*.

## What Is Anytime Coaching?

Anytime Coaching is a set of practices that enables those in leadership positions to guide the people doing the work while unleashing their best thinking and growing their overall competence. Anytime Coaching creates day-to-day shifts in employee competence that—over time—yield improved individual and organizational performance. Anytime Coaching is a way of understanding and interacting with others so that forward motion is the focus, future outcomes are the goals, and ongoing personal growth is the result. You can incorporate Anytime Coaching practices in your daily duties as a supervisor, manager, team lead, project manager, or any position where you are shaping the work and behavior of others.

## How Does Anytime Coaching Differ from Other Types of Coaching?

With Anytime Coaching, the manager sees daily interactions with employees as "coachable" moments. The anytime coach's conversations foster independent thought, creativity, and employee growth—all while improving performance bit by bit, day by day. The anytime coach does not reserve coaching solely for problems and breakdowns. A manager may set appointments for special coaching conversations at challenging times; the anytime coach reduces the need for such problem-focused talks through skillful coaching *anytime*.

## When Does Anytime Coaching Happen?

Once an employee has the basic skills to perform his or her job, as well as an understanding of the job itself and its contribution to the bigger picture, Anytime Coaching can happen *at any time* during the workday. Anytime Coaching happens when an employee is challenged to develop new abilities, gain deeper understanding, make difficult decisions and tradeoffs, or exercise new skills to tackle obstacles, small and large—on the way to getting good work done. Managers can provide Anytime Coaching when the inevitable changes, obstacles, confusion, and questions arise as work is done.

Anytime Coaching happens—needs to happen—in situations like the following:

- An employee's understanding of the job is challenged by others.
- An employee's peer fails to deliver information required for the employee to do the job well.
- The input provided is not what is expected, or it is late.
- Resources shrink or disappear, making daily work more difficult.
- An employee is not completing day-to-day tasks on time.
- Organizational priorities change.
- An employee realizes he or she has more tasks than seem possible to accomplish in the time allotted.
- What the employee produces does not match expectations.
- A deadline is missed.
- Things do not go as promised.

These and a whole host of other daily challenges are starting points for Anytime Coaching.

Let's not forget that Anytime Coaching also happens when there is good news. When an employee solves a difficult problem independently or consistently delivers excellent performance, an anytime coach makes sure to recognize and reinforce the positive outcomes. This means delivering more than a simple compliment like "Nice job!" Anytime coaches notice positive actions and take the time to say, "Here is what I see you doing, and here is why it is appreciated." Linking specific skills and behaviors with positive reinforcement encourages improved performance. Anytime coaches keep a balance in their employee conversations between positive reinforcement and change-oriented coaching.

## Coaching, Not Telling

Anytime Coaching is not the same as telling people what to do. Certainly, part of a manager's job is to explain to an employee what the job entails and how the job is connected to the organization's overall purpose. This "telling" is indeed part of what managers *must* do to establish performance standards and delegate work in support of larger goals. For many managers, it is all too tempting (and seemingly expedient) to continue the "telling" whenever a question or problem arises. Certainly, there are times—especially in emergencies and under tight deadlines—when a leader-driven solution might be the best alternative.

One of the challenges for managers developing Anytime Coaching skills is learning when "telling" is the best course and when coaching will prompt better—and more sustainable—performance.

## The Anytime Coaching Model

The Anytime Coaching model comprises four interrelated practices: observing, inquiring, listening, and responding. At the center of the model is what the practices achieve: day-to-day performance improvement. Supporting and surrounding the four practices are four other elements: the coach's self- and organizational awareness, a commitment to ongoing personal growth and development, increased awareness of the growing body of knowledge in neuroscience, and an attitude of mindfulness.

The model is dynamic in that the four practices are interrelated and dependent. An anytime coach interweaves observing, inquiring, listening, and responding into powerful conversations that cause

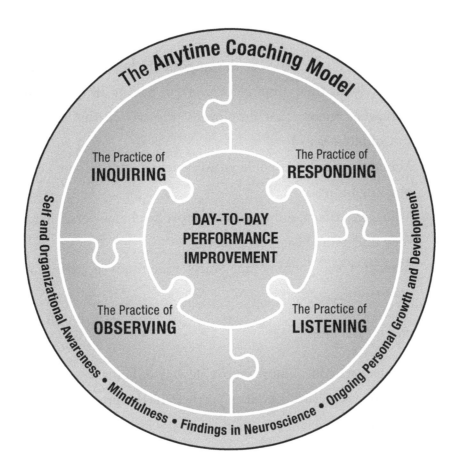

day-to-day shifts in employee performance. As the anytime coach's self-awareness and organizational awareness expand, so does his or her skill in using the four practices. The expanding knowledge of neuroscience continues to support anecdotal wisdom with fact-based findings. The anytime coach who cultivates a practice of mindfulness engages others in a calm, centered, and focused manner.

The path to Anytime Coaching is an ongoing journey, full of opportunities to continually refine skills and achieve mastery.

## ▪▪▪ Anytime Coaching Outcomes

When you practice Anytime Coaching, you will witness numerous positive outcomes for the manager, the employee, and the organization.

*Outcomes for the manager:*

- Managers no longer bear the impossible burden of being the expert about their employees' work or having all the answers.
- Managers ensure that employees' responsibilities stay with the employees.
- Managers see their people grow, develop, and become capable of doing more.
- Managers trust their employees more (and vice versa) because they understand each other better.
- Managers see incremental shifts in employee performance over time.

*Outcomes for the employee:*

- Being coached is a more enjoyable way of being managed.
- Employees feel respected as partners in the process of getting work done.
- Employees' competence improves day by day; as a result, so does performance.
- Employees know what their responsibilities are and feel empowered to fulfill them.
- Employees make decisions based on their own best thinking.
- Employees exercise more creativity in how they meet organizational requirements.
- Employees are more likely to ask questions to ensure they are doing the right thing.
- Employees are less fearful and more capable of appropriate risk-taking.

*Outcomes for the organization:*

■ Anytime Coaching creates an environment of collaboration and cooperation between layers of management and among peers at all levels.

■ Anytime Coaching unlocks employees' internal motivations and fosters a sense of well-being at work and, as a result, greater productivity for the organization.

■ With Anytime Coaching as a way of life, organizations experience more job satisfaction and less turnover.

■ The small daily shifts in employee performance lead to improved overall organizational performance.

## Why Does Anytime Coaching Work?

Anytime Coaching skills are powerful and effective for a variety of reasons. The skills leverage recent findings in the fields of neuroscience, emotional intelligence, leadership development, human resource management, organizational development, positive psychology, and mindfulness.

Work in the field of neuroscience confirms what many of us already know: When people figure something out on their own (even with help), they "own" it. And now, neuroscience tells us that their brain pathways are changed in a way that embeds the learning and makes it more likely to be repeated.[1] "Neuroplasticity" describes how the brain reorganizes neural pathways based on new experience. As we gain new knowledge and skills, our brain creates new neural connections, enabling us to grow and develop. Anytime Coaching works because it fosters and encourages sustainable change within ourselves as well as our employees.

People who do only what they are told to do lack opportunities to grow through experimentation and reliance on their own judgment, experience, and hunches. People willingly exercise their own judgment, experience, and hunches when they know such behavior is both expected and respected. When managed by supervisors with good coaching skills, people perform better, learn more, and grow in overall competence and confidence—and the organization enjoys better results.

Neuroscience also explains why learning the four Anytime Coaching practices requires focus. The brain has two systems that are in constant competition for our attention and awareness. The first system is the higher, more rational, calmer system known as the prefrontal cortex. Think of the prefrontal cortex as the brain's executive front office or C-suite. The prefrontal lobes allow for higher levels of planning, reasoning, remaining rational, and staying calm. A second brain system, the limbic system, relies on more primitive, deeply embedded cortical networks. The limbic system is often referred to as the emotional system of the brain because it "tracks your emotional relationship to thoughts, objects, people and events"[2] and it is where emotional memory is stored. This more primitive, fast-acting system often leads to ineffective management choices and snap judgments compared to the higher level, well-thought out executive brain system.

Becoming an anytime coach enables you to gain better access to the prefrontal cortex and its front-office capabilities such as strategizing and planning, while quieting the limbic system.

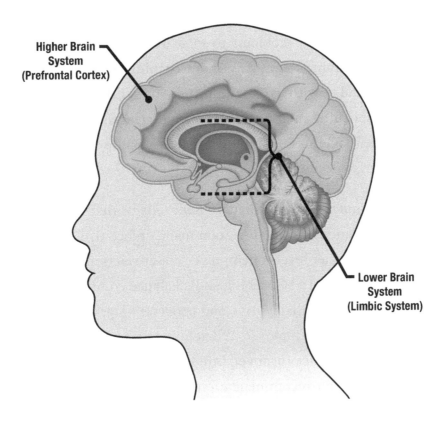

Higher Brain
System
(Prefrontal Cortex)

Lower Brain
System
(Limbic System)

Work in the field of emotional intelligence tells us that career success depends less on knowledge and expertise in a particular discipline and more on interpersonal relationships and social skills.[3] Coaching behaviors help managers who are experts in their fields interact with peers and subordinates in ways that honor everyone's contribution to the work at hand and that develop new experts. When leaders' interpersonal and social skills include the art of Anytime Coaching, they actively develop new leaders.

Experts whose job it is to develop leaders have found that leadership takes many forms, and people can lead from wherever they are in the organization. When leaders coach, their people step forward into challenging situations to present new options and solutions, and they are treated respectfully when they do. Risk-taking and potential failure are seen as part of the learning process. People grow when they are given difficult problems to solve along with the latitude to be creative in solving them. Anytime Coaching skills help a leader decide when and how to work with people so that they become leaders in accomplishing their own work. Such increased self-awareness is a component of emotionally intelligent leadership, which anytime coaches learn to develop.

Research in human resource management tells us that organizations with an abundance of top-down, command-and-control managerial practices have higher levels of employee dissatisfaction and turnover and lower productivity.[4] Coaching skills balance command-and-control behaviors with collaborative and cooperative practices that engage the best of every employee. When human resource professionals are asked how to reduce turnover, improve morale, and boost productivity, many of their recommendations center on changing managerial behavior. Those recommendations include training managers in many of the skills we call Anytime Coaching.

Organizational development experts tell us that groups of people working together naturally form accepted ways of behaving, and that what becomes accepted is greatly influenced by those in power positions.[5] When managers adopt Anytime Coaching as a business-as-usual system of managing, the influence is felt throughout the organization. People know what they are supposed to do and know they are seen as competent and growing individuals whose contributions are necessary and vital to the organization. While the organizational chart may still look like a top-down arrangement, the behaviors between levels of management and across peer groups become coaching-based. Gone are fears of blame and punishment; in their place are risk tolerance, collaboration, shared credit, and responsibility. Anytime Coaching skills help create this type of positive workplace reality.

The field of positive psychology continues to provide evidence that people at work are happier and do better work when they (1) are appreciated for their unique skills and abilities, (2) have opportunities to use those skills and abilities in ways that generate positive outcomes, (3) are given opportunities to learn and develop new competencies, and (4) are recognized appropriately for their efforts and achievements. Anytime Coaching skills provide managers the tools and techniques necessary to interact with employees in ways that create a positive work climate where people know they are valued and, as a result, willingly share their value with the organization and continue to grow.

Research in the field of mindfulness has found that the regular practice of focusing on the present, allowing distracting thoughts to pass on by, has the benefit of increasing our ability to regain that focus throughout daily activities. From the perspective of neuroscience, mindfulness can be characterized "as a series of mental exercises by which one strengthens one's control over the workings of their own brains."[6] Becoming more mindful creates a more resilient supervisor, manager, or employee, able to weather workplace challenges without becoming overly anxious, overwhelmed, or paralyzed by doubt or fear. By developing a sense of calm, clarity, and "focus on the moment," the anytime coach minimizes distractions when observing and interacting with others. Through Anytime Coaching, you will learn ways to be more present, more aware, and more focused.

## ▪▪▪ Can I Learn Anytime Coaching?

The answer is "Yes!" Anytime Coaching rests on basic skills you already have: observing, inquiring, listening, and responding. You will develop Anytime Coaching skills when you look at such routine activities with new eyes—when you leave your comfort zone and expand your natural abilities and skills. Observing will become far more than just looking around you. Inquiring will become more than a series of "whys." Listening will become more than just hearing an employee's words. Responding will become an act of creating intentional conversation. When your daily work conversations include all these Anytime Coaching practices, you will enable employees to tap into their own knowledge, create their own solutions, develop new abilities, and improve performance.

Anyone can learn Anytime Coaching; it all begins with you.

## NOTES

1. David Rock, *Quiet Leadership* (New York: Collins Business, 2006), pp. 3–6.

2. David Rock, *Your Brain at Work* (New York: HarperCollins, 2009), p. 103.

3. Daniel Goleman, *Working with Emotional Intelligence* (New York: Bantam Books, 1998), pp. 18–29. Also, Michael M. Lombardo and Robert W. Eichinger, *Preventing Derailment: What to Do Before It's Too Late* (Greensboro, NC: CCL Press, 1989), pp. 4–11; and Jean Brittain, Leslie Van Velsor, and Ellen Van Velsor, *A Look at Derailment Today: North America and Europe* (Greensboro, NC: CCL Press, 1996), pp. 14–17.

4. Daniel Goleman, Richard Boyatzis, and Annie McKee, *Primal Leadership: Realizing the Power of Emotional Intelligence* (Boston: Harvard Business School Press, 2002), pp. 76–79. Also, Dan Baker, Cathy Greenberg, and Collins Hemingway, *What Happy Companies Know* (Upper Saddle River, NJ: Pearson Prentice Hall, 2006), p. 223.

5. Daniel Goleman, Richard Boyatzis, and Annie McKee, *Primal Leadership: Realizing the Power of Emotional Intelligence* (Boston: Harvard Business School Press, 2002), p. 251. Also, Daniel Goleman, Richard Boyatsis, and Annie McKee, "Primal Leadership: The Hidden Driver of Great Performance," *Harvard Business Review*, December 2001, pp. 45–47.

6. Peter B. Reiner, "Meditation on Demand," *Scientific American*, May 26, 2009. *www.scientificamerican.com.*

## RECOMMENDED READING

Anchor, Shawn. *The Happiness Advantage: The Seven Principles of Positive Psychology That Fuel Success and Performance at Work.* New York: Crown Business, 2010.

Goleman, Daniel. *Focus: The Hidden Driver of Excellence.* New York: HarperCollins, 2013.

Kabat-Zinn, Jon. *Mindfulness for Beginners.* Boulder, CO: Sounds True Inc., 2012.

Kabat-Zinn, Jon. *Wherever You Go, There You Are.* New York: Hyperion, 1994 and 2005.

Kahneman, Daniel. *Thinking, Fast and Slow.* New York: Farrar, Straus and Giroux, 2011.

Rock, David. *Quiet Leadership.* New York: Collins Business, 2006.

# 1 It All Begins with You

> "We must be the change we wish to see in the world."
> —MAHATMA GANDHI, INDIAN SPIRITUAL AND POLITICAL INDEPENDENCE LEADER

As a well-known saying goes, "No matter where you go, there you are." Amusing and paradoxical as it may be, the saying is true. After all, it is you who shows up at work every day and you who returns home, listens to music, watches a movie, or goes out with friends. Learning more about yourself is a good starting point for your journey as an anytime coach. What you learn will add to, modify, or replace beliefs, knowledge, and skills you have now.

We first ask you to think deeply about the "self" you bring to Anytime Coaching. You will complete several informal self-assessments that focus on your beliefs about work and managing others, as well as your skills, knowledge, and preferences. Then we encourage you to reflect on what you have discovered. You might even want to retake the assessments once you have implemented some of the Anytime Coaching practices.[1]

Undoubtedly, you already use some of the skills of Anytime Coaching. As the Anytime Coaching model depicts, the core practices of observing, inquiring, listening, and responding are linked to one another. When anytime coaches employ all four practices, the result is day-to-day performance improvement. Surrounding and supporting these four practices are the additional elements of self-awareness, self-development, neuroscience, and mindfulness.

## ▪ ▪ ▪ Who Is the Self I Bring to Anytime Coaching?

Each individual will answer this question differently—but do take some time to answer it. The self-assessments will help you determine your current skills and beliefs, which will influence how you adopt and apply Anytime Coaching skills. The immediate goal is to boost your understanding of your skill as an employee, a manager, or a leader. There will be no "score" for the assessments—just increased awareness of the self you bring to Anytime Coaching.

To begin, the exercises ask that you think deeply about your work, your beliefs about work, your workplace, your employees, and your role as a manager. You will base your new learning about Anytime Coaching on these core beliefs.

## ▪ ▪ ▪ Thinking about Work

As we understand more about brain development, we have come to realize that thoughts profoundly impact our feelings, emotions, and actions through the brain's release of powerful neurochemicals. That is why taking time to think about work is our starting point—to help you gain understanding of your feelings about your work and about being an anytime coach. What are your thoughts about paid work in general? Do you view work as providing opportunities for creativity, or does it seem merely routine? Do you think mostly about the problems immediately before you, or are you able to envision the future?

Our first jobs, our parents' work experiences, anecdotes from others about their jobs, and our personal preferences all contribute to our beliefs about what work is and why we do it. People who see work as part of a larger pattern in their lives—as a means for making a contribution, getting recognition for a job well done, or developing personal strengths—will find that Anytime Coaching skills are relevant to both the practical side of work (completing tasks and being paid) and its more personal aspects (such as professional growth and fulfillment). If we tend to think of work as simply a burden to be endured so that we can pay the bills, we may view Anytime Coaching skills as a way to transform our work.

"I had chosen my work as a reflection of my values."

—SIDNEY POITIER, AMERICAN ACTOR

#### ■ ■ ■ ■ ■  EXERCISE
#### How You View Your Work

Of the words and phrases below, circle seven to ten that come to mind when you think about the work you do. If you do not see seven to ten words or phrases that describe your thoughts, write your choice of words in the space provided.

*My View of Work*

valuable     fun     drudgery     follow orders     exciting     routine     interesting
depressing     challenging     just a necessity     tolerable     stimulating     educational
fulfilling     frustrating     path to promotion     beneficial     amusing     complicated
stressful     teamwork     just a paycheck     great people     confusing     inspiring
chaos     collegial     visionary     creative     lively     dull     energizing     right balance
overwhelming     tedious     opportunity to grow     pressure     invigorating     taxing     tense
boring     happy     lots of overtime     difficult     worthwhile     easy     my life's purpose
too much to do     stagnant     satisfying     problems     fascinating     time well spent
engaging     intimidating     camaraderie     just a small part of my life     rewarding
tiring

_____

_____

_____

_____

### ▓ ▓  Thinking about Your Role as a Manager

Anyone who has held a job has also had a boss. Whether your early working experiences were positive or negative will influence your own behavior when it is your turn to lead others. The management training you have had has likely influenced your understanding of your role too. And of course, your relationship with your own manager will have a direct effect on how you interact with your employees.

To manage others most effectively, you must be confident in your own beliefs but also open to new behaviors and attitudes. Whether you are a "command and control" manager or friendly and affable, learning new skills will test what you already believe. Most people who manage the work of others find that they must create a balance between motivating employees to do what is required and to proactively and continuously seek and develop creative solutions that fit ever-changing circumstances.

■ ■ ■ ■ ■ **EXERCISE**
### How You View Your Role as a Manager

Think about your specific duties as a manager of others. Circle seven to ten words or phrases that most readily come to mind when you think about your management responsibilities. If you do not see seven to ten words or phrases that describe your thoughts, write your choice of words in the space provided.

The words and phrases below are the same as those in the previous exercise, but this time make your selections based specifically on what it is like to be a manager.

***My View of Being a Manager***
valuable    fun    drudgery    follow orders    exciting    routine    interesting
depressing    challenging    just a necessity    tolerable    stimulating    educational
fulfilling    frustrating    path to promotion    beneficial    amusing    complicated
stressful    teamwork    just a paycheck    great people    confusing    inspiring
chaos    collegial    visionary    creative    lively    dull    energizing    right balance
overwhelming    tedious    opportunity to grow    pressure    invigorating    taxing    tense
boring    happy    lots of overtime    difficult    worthwhile    easy    my life's purpose
too much to do    stagnant    satisfying    problems    fascinating    time well spent
engaging    intimidating    camaraderie    just a small part of my life    rewarding
tiring

_____

_____

_____

_____

What do you notice about the similarity or dissimilarity of the words you circled to describe your attitude toward work in general and those you circled above? How would you explain the similarity or difference?

_____

_____

_____

_____

## ▪ ▪ Thinking about Your Skills, Knowledge, and Preferences

An accurate assessment of your skill level, knowledge base, and preferences in social and work styles will help you as you learn the skills of Anytime Coaching. Reflecting on your own thinking will also impact your feelings, thoughts, and motivations as you learn new coaching practices.

Even if some coaching skills are new to you, you are likely to succeed if you are committed to learning them. And if you are able to acknowledge freely that you do not have all the answers at work (even though you might be the boss), learning Anytime Coaching skills will help you get the best from everyone else's knowledge and expertise.

When it comes to personal preferences in work and social styles, simply being aware of your tendencies can be helpful. For example, if you are naturally gregarious and outgoing, you may decide to be less talkative to build your listening skills. Or if you strive for speed at all costs, you may learn a lot just by slowing down to have in-depth coaching conversations. Running at an overwhelmed, frenzied pace with excessive stress triggers a powerful neurochemical called cortisol. Over time, excess stress and cortisol can take a toll on your body, thinking, and memory. As we will explore in Chapter 2, you can improve your ability to slow down by integrating simple practices for being more present, aware, and focused in your day-to-day work.

Complete the following exercise to gain insight into how you view your own skills, knowledge, and preferences.

■ ■ ■ ■ ■ **EXERCISE**
## How You View Your Skills, Knowledge, and Preferences

**Skills and Knowledge.** Assess your proficiency in each of the following skills. Check the most appropriate box beside each statement.

|  | Excellent | Good | Satisfactory | Less than Satisfactory | Unacceptable |
|---|---|---|---|---|---|
| My ability to perform the technical aspects of my job |  |  |  |  |  |
| My subject-matter expertise |  |  |  |  |  |
| My skills in managing others |  |  |  |  |  |
| My interpersonal skills |  |  |  |  |  |
| My ability to observe others |  |  |  |  |  |
| My ability to listen deeply |  |  |  |  |  |
| My ability to respond to others in a way appropriate to the situation |  |  |  |  |  |
| My ability to ask powerful questions |  |  |  |  |  |
| My ability to influence employee performance |  |  |  |  |  |

**Preferences.** How well does each listed behavior or attitude describe you at work? Check the most appropriate box beside each statement.

|  | Most of the time | Some of the time | Not very often |
|---|---|---|---|
| I prefer to work in groups of people |  |  |  |
| I am better as an individual contributor |  |  |  |
| I can work equally well in groups or alone |  |  |  |
| I deal with conflict situations calmly |  |  |  |
| I avoid conflict |  |  |  |
| I can deal with conflict if I have to |  |  |  |
| I voice my opinions freely |  |  |  |
| I show interest in others' ideas |  |  |  |
| I ask a lot of questions |  |  |  |
| I can persuade people easily |  |  |  |
| I can sense what people are feeling |  |  |  |
| I show my emotions freely |  |  |  |
| I look at the big picture |  |  |  |
| I am fond of details |  |  |  |
| I like logical decision-making |  |  |  |
| I tend to feel my way to a decision |  |  |  |
| I care if people approve of my work |  |  |  |
| I care if people like me |  |  |  |
| I get things done quickly |  |  |  |
| I take my time to complete tasks |  |  |  |

## ■ ■ ■ Thinking about Your Organization

Assessing your organization's approach to getting work done is an important step as you begin to try out new coaching behaviors. As a worker, you operate within a network of other workers. Some are your peers, some are "above" you in the hierarchy, and some may be "below" you. Organizations in which hierarchically driven behavior is pervasive and ingrained may be less hospitable to some coaching behaviors. In contrast, workplaces in which people at all levels mingle freely, sharing ideas up and down the chain, may be more open to Anytime Coaching. Practicing what you learn is essential, so it is helpful to be aware of the culture of your work environment.

How you see your own work and your role as a worker, your skills/ knowledge/preferences, and your organizational culture will influence every coaching conversation you have. These elements are the foundation on which every coaching conversation rests. As your understanding of each deepens, you can begin to build the skills that will make you a successful anytime coach in your particular environment.

■ ■ ■ ■ ■  **EXERCISE**
## How You View Your Organization

Think about how people work and interact in your organization. To what degree do you believe each statement below describes your workplace?

| | Agree strongly | Somewhat agree | Neither agree nor disagree | Somewhat disagree | Disagree strongly |
|---|---|---|---|---|---|
| People are interested in finding better ways to work | | | | | |
| The culture supports finding the best solutions | | | | | |
| We operate within a strict chain-of-command hierarchy | | | | | |
| New ideas are shared widely and are discussed by many | | | | | |
| My organization makes a positive difference in the lives of those who work here | | | | | |
| My organization wants people to have a chance to grow while in their jobs | | | | | |
| My organization does not tolerate poor work for long | | | | | |
| You are expected to be on top of your game and know the answers at all times | | | | | |
| It's OK to say "I don't know" | | | | | |
| People are encouraged to try new things and to take risks | | | | | |
| Most employees want to do a good job | | | | | |

■ ■ ■ ■ ■   **EXERCISE**
## Reflection

Reflect on the insights you have gained from examining how you view work; your role as a manager; your skills, knowledge, and preferences; and your organization. Take the time now to capture what you noticed about yourself and these four areas. To summarize your discoveries, complete each sentence below:

When I think of work, I generally think that. . .

_____

_____

_____

When I think about managing people, I believe. . .

_____

_____

_____

When I think about my own skills, knowledge, and preferences:

   I know I am good at. . .

   _____

   _____

   I know I need to improve. . .

   _____

   _____

   I know my preferences help me. . .

   _____

   _____

   I know my preferences may hinder me in. . .

   _____

   _____

When I think about the organization where I work, I believe that. . .

_____

_____

_____

## ▪▪▪ **The Practices of Anytime Coaching**

In the chapters ahead, we will talk about the key practices of Any-time Coaching. The word "practices" is significant here. A practice is something you do regularly, with the goal of continual, broad im-provement. For example, a pianist practices scales and finger exercises to build greater facility in playing sonatas and concertos. A basketball player practices dribbling and hook shots to develop particular skills essential to playing the game well. We know from neuroscience that creating habits through practice is fundamental to forging powerful new neural connections. You too must practice individual skills to be successful in the game of Anytime Coaching.

What do you practice? The key practices are observing, inquiring, lis-tening, and responding. What happens when you employ all these skills effectively? Day-to-day performance improvement.

Let's begin with the practice of observing.

---

**NOTE**

1. Many widely used self-assessment instruments provide more in-depth interpretation of your results. These include the Myers-Briggs Type Indicator®, the FIRO-B®, and the DISC® assessments. For the Myers-Briggs Type Indicator® and the FIRO-B®, visit *www.cpp.com*. For the DISC® instrument, visit *www.everythingdisc.com*.

# 2 The Practice of Observing

"Accuracy of observation is the equivalent of accuracy of thinking."

—WALLACE STEVENS, AMERICAN POET

Now that you know that coaching begins with you, as the manager or team lead, you are ready to begin exploring the practices of Anytime Coaching. These practices will guide you in creating new ways of interacting with your employees—ways that enhance their performance and your relationships with them. You will learn and use new and powerful approaches to observing, inquiring, listening, and responding.

Our first stop is the practice of observing, because it is by observing that you create an effective foundation for all the other practices.

## ■ ■ ■ The Powerful Practice of Observing

What is the practice of observing? *Webster's New World Dictionary* defines observing as "the act, practice, or power of noticing." Observing requires you to accurately and objectively notice the people, activities, events, and communication around you with a fresh perspective. Through close observation, you will notice qualities in your employees you may have missed before, and you will pay closer attention to nonverbal cues and emotions. The practice of observing intensifies, widens, and deepens your focus.

Staying outwardly focused and observing employees takes intentional focus and practice. Staying focused may sound simple, but your brain circuits make it difficult. The brain is easily distracted and quickly moves to default mode, in which thoughts turn inward. The brain also has an innate, natural bias toward negative thoughts, which evolved to ensure our survival and safety but makes staying neutral and observing others more challenging.

With shorter deadlines, mounting pressure to maintain a rapid pace, and constant technological changes, the powerful practice of observing is even more critical in today's overwhelmed and stressed workplace. What occurs when employees face chronic pressure and stress? Does it feel harder to stay calm and access the important executive-suite brain system during your workday?

"When stress becomes more than an occasional burst, when it becomes a constant, grinding swirl... feeling behind, jumping from task to task and never feeling there is time to do everything you have to do... [neuroscientists] are finding the prefrontal cortex begins to shut down. The more stress, scans show, the smaller volume of neuron-rich gray matter in this key region of the brain."[1]

The practice of observing is an effective way to counter the impact on the brain of what we call "cognitive capacity overload." Cognitive overload occurs when your brain is flooded with incoming thoughts or information and you feel overwhelmed. "You have to consistently apply your frontal lobes to help you, or any progress will be hit and miss. It's very easy when you are living in a rushing, reactive mode to have the frontal lobes all but drowned out by the doom-and-gloom brain regions that clamor for attention and can flood your body with stress chemicals at the slightest bit of pressure or foreshadowing of change."[2]

As you develop as an anytime coach, you will learn that observing is an essential foundation for the other skills outlined in the Anytime Coaching model. For example, observing leads to asking powerful questions. Your questions will be based on what you notice as you observe your employees' verbal and nonverbal communication. Observing complements listening; as you move beyond merely hearing what employees say, you will practice a deeper form of listening that yields more information. Observing also allows you to respond to your employees in the most appropriate way. Finally, observing helps you notice opportunities for results-focused Anytime Coaching—and results are, of course, the ultimate goal of your coaching conversations.

Why is observing a powerful practice for Anytime Coaching? First, observing employees' best qualities (a new practice for many managers) helps build a positive foundation for employee-manager interactions. You will find that observing the positive leads to greater collaboration, commitment, and trust in your working relationships.

Second, observing enables you to learn significant details about your employees. You will notice verbal, nonverbal, and emotional cues and will likely find that your employees have interests and capabilities of which you were not aware and that can be explored during your coaching. Finally, self-observation will help you understand your own style and preferences when interacting with others. This is particularly important if your management style is more directive than collaborative—if you tend to tell more than ask.

You will learn how to engage in the practice of observing in four ways:

1. *Observing positive qualities and possibilities in your employees.* Employees' good qualities and potential too often go unnoticed. We offer techniques to help you change how you observe your employees and uncover positive possibilities.

2. *Observing nonverbal cues and the emotions underlying employees' words.* What role do these play in communication? We provide exercises to help you decode the clues. We also discuss the importance of congruence between verbal, vocal, and visual communication and of becoming a nonjudgmental observer.

3. *Observing whether you have a tendency to direct, not coach.* We help you notice whether you often tell others what to do instead of coaching. We urge you to take note of your impatient, performance-oriented "fast results gene" (FRG) and explain how to tame it, allowing you to coach more effectively.

4. *Observing your mindful presence.* We describe how being more present, aware, and focused will improve your observation abilities—of others and yourself. To help you become more familiar with mindfulness, we provide short, practical exercises and suggest some reference materials. These mindfulness exercises will

help you become more present, aware, and focused as an anytime coach.

We begin the practice of observing by focusing on positive possibilities in others.

■ ■ ■ ■ ■ ■ ■ ■ ■

> "The person who sends out positive thoughts activates the world around him positively and draws back to himself positive results."
>
> —NORMAN VINCENT PEALE, AUTHOR OF *THE POWER OF POSITIVE THINKING*

■ ■ ■ ■ ■ ■ ■ ■ ■

## Observing Positive Qualities and Possibilities in Your Employees

Rather than focusing on employees' weaknesses, look at the larger picture. Think about what each employee does well and how his or her work style is effective. This sounds simple, but observing positive qualities takes focus and practice.

Why is it hard to look for positive possibilities in others? Managers generally are not trained in or rewarded for observing the positive. Instead, most managers are skilled at, and rewarded for, solving problems. They pay attention to what is not working and fix it. There is less apparent short-term incentive to ask: "What is working really well with my employees, and how can I build on their strengths?"

Managers get very comfortable, perhaps too comfortable, observing a situation or an employee through the lens of problem solving. They then perceive their employees as problems that need fixing or improvement. It becomes easy and automatic to ask: "How did this employee not meet performance expectations?" "What does this person lack?"

We believe it is a huge shift in perspective to *first* notice your employees' positive qualities and *then* determine what can be improved. When you do so, the positive qualities and possibilities you notice may seem simple. But they are important building blocks, and observing good qualities is an essential aspect of becoming an anytime coach.

This practice of observing positive qualities in your employees and others also yields favorable neural rewards that "activate brain centers that open you up to new possibilities."[3] Daniel Goleman summarizes the benefits of following a positive approach:

> *A focus on our strengths urges us toward a desired future and stimulates openness to new ideas, people and plans. In contrast, spotlighting our weaknesses elicits a defensive sense of obligation and guilt, closing us down. The positive lens keeps the joy in practice and learning—the reason even the most seasoned athletes still enjoy rehearsing their moves. You need the negative focus to survive, but a positive one to thrive.*[4]

Observing is how you begin to notice the potential in others and find possibilities for them.

### ▨ ▨ Getting Started in Observing Positives

Here are some examples of positive qualities to look for in each of your employees:

- ▨ Does this person work hard? Put in long hours?
- ▨ Is he or she punctual?
- ▨ Is he or she trustworthy?
- ▨ Is he or she modest and humble?

- Is his or her work detailed or thorough?
- Does he or she perform well when working in a group?
- Does he or she take feedback well?
- Does he or she have a sense of humor?

#### ■ ■ ■ ■ ■ ■  PRINCIPLE

Anytime coaches notice their employees' positive qualities and look for positive possibilities in them.

The following scenario illustrates the power of seeing an employee with new eyes and the possibilities created by doing so.

### ▨ ▨  Observing with a New Perspective: Mark and Pat's Story

When Mark, a manager, joins the organization, he inherits Pat, an unmotivated, underperforming employee. The previous manager had given up on Pat. But Mark sees Pat with new eyes and a fresh perspective. Mark notices Pat's verbal and nonverbal communication and tries to observe her emotions. She is very quiet, withdrawn, and nervous during team meetings. Mark sees Pat not as someone who lacks motivation, but as a person with unrealized potential.

As Mark coaches and encourages her, Pat's work begins to improve within a few months. Everyone in the department is surprised by Pat's strong performance, and the team dubs Mark a "turnaround" manager. But Mark is not a "turnaround" manager. He simply tries to see people in a positive light, looking for potential and opportunity in everyone through the practice of observing.

## ▨ ▨ ▨  Seeing with New Eyes

When a new manager brings a different perspective to a workplace, employees respond by coming alive and achieving better results. Such opportunities await the anytime coach, beginning with the practice of observing.

How did Mark observe positive possibilities in Pat? He noticed that Pat was painfully shy, very quiet, and overly detail-oriented. The previous manager thought these qualities were a problem in a team setting. But Mark saw tremendous potential in Pat that could benefit her as well as the team. For example, she could do project analysis by herself, taking the time to dig into the details. She could write up reports on her findings but not be required to attend frequent team meetings, where she froze up. When Pat was encouraged to do this critical, detailed analytical work, she was thrilled and she thrived in her position.

By focusing on your employees' positive qualities and what *is* working, you will notice possibilities for them that you overlooked before. You may find they have skills or talents that you had not noticed. Tasks that build on an employee's strengths and gifts may become obvious. Positive possibilities—maybe finding new ways to get a job done or coming up with innovative methods for tackling a problem—can be explored and discussed in coaching conversations.

■ ■ ■ ■ ■ ■ ■ ■ ■ ■

"When you change the way you look at things, the things you look at change."

—MAX PLANCK, GERMAN PHYSICIST

■ ■ ■ ■ ■ ■ ■ ■ ■ ■

### Checklist of Positive Questions

The following checklist of questions will help you look for positive qualities and possibilities in others:

- What does this employee do well?
- What are his or her strengths?
- What do I appreciate most about this person?

■ What strengths do others see in this employee that I, as the manager, may miss?

■ What unique attributes does this person bring to the workplace?

■ What positive work habits does this employee have?

---

■ ■ ■ ■ ■ **PRACTICE TOOL**
**Observing Your Employees**

This practice tool will help you focus on observing your employees' positive qualities.

Think of a specific employee. You may want to select someone you do not know very well or an employee with whom you have had past difficulties.

Name: _____

Write down three to five positive qualities the employee exhibits or things he or she does well. Then, look for evidence of these positive traits and record your observations.

| I believe [employee] has the following qualities: | I observe this when he or she ... |
| --- | --- |
| Positive Quality 1 | |
| Positive Quality 2 | |
| Positive Quality 3 | |
| Positive Quality 4 | |
| Positive Quality 5 | |

### Changing Your Observation Lens

Here's what can happen when you try observing a situation with a challenging employee in three different ways, including focusing on positive possibilities.

When problems at work arise, a lawyer with more than 25 years of experience has a habit of saying, "We tried that in the past, and it will never work." This attorney is perceived as cynical and critical, and his behavior irritates the younger attorneys working on his team, who like to come up with new ideas and suggestions.

Imagine that you are the experienced attorney's manager. Here are three possible lenses through which you could observe him.

**Observing Lens 1: Inaction.** "This old-timer is a complainer who will not change or try anything different. I will tell the younger team members to ignore him, and they will just have to stay frustrated until he retires. That is how things work around here."

**Observing Lens 2: Exclusion.** "This older lawyer is a problem employee who is only focused on retirement. My only choice is to keep him away from others to get him out of the picture. I will avoid him at all costs. I will not invite him to meetings, or I will talk over him so that younger team members do not get frustrated and leave for another division. I will also stop copying him on my emails."

**Observing Lens 3: Positive possibilities.** "The attorney is an older employee who has tremendous experience and insider knowledge. It could benefit younger employees to gain institutional memory from him. Of course, his focus is on retirement and leaving, so he is less interested in innovation and change. That is natural and normal. Even so, I think he is a positive addition to our legal team, and I want to find out as much as possible from him about why we did not implement changes in the past. What would he have done differently as an advisor to the new project to help ensure its success? I want to learn more about him, so I will use Anytime Coaching skills to find out more. I will talk to him privately, outside of meetings."

"The pessimist sees difficulty in every opportunity. The optimist sees the opportunity in every difficulty."

—WINSTON CHURCHILL, FORMER BRITISH PRIME MINISTER

## The Positive Principle

Looking for positive possibilities in your employees can affect the entire workplace, not just your work as an anytime coach. Numerous researchers[5] have studied the physical and emotional benefits of seeking out the positive:

> *Given the negativity bias of the brain it takes an active effort to internalize positive experiences and heal negative ones.... Focusing on what is whole and then taking it in naturally increases the positive emotions flowing through your mind each day. Emotions have a global effect since they organize the brain as a whole. Consequently, positive feelings have far-reaching benefits, including a stronger immune system and a cardiovascular system that is less reactive to stress. They lift your mood, increase optimism, resiliency and resourcefulness.[6]*

In short, the positive principle of Anytime Coaching truly helps people feel good.

Dr. David Cooperrider and his colleagues at Case Western Reserve University have studied the significant effects of observing positive possibilities on both individual and workplace effectiveness, especially during times of change. Cooperrider is best known as one of the founders of appreciative inquiry, a highly successful facilitation and organizational development approach that "searches for the best in people, their organizations and the relevant world around them."[7] Cooperrider writes: "The Positive Principle... is not so abstract.... I have found it does not help, in the long run, to begin my inquiries from the standpoint of the world as a problem to be solved. I am more effective, quite simply, as long as I can retain the spirit of inquiry of the everlasting beginner."[8]

Another example comes from research in the field of positive psychology, which underscores the need for creating positive interactions with others, largely based on noticing an individual's good qualities and potential. Researchers Tom Rath and Donald Clifton of the Gallup Organization have studied the importance of frequent, small positive acts in motivating others and getting results. Rath and Clifton have found that a "Magic Ratio of 3 positive interactions for every 1 negative interaction"[9] is effective. The researchers explain that "the positivity must be grounded in reality. A Pollyanna approach, in which the negative is completely ignored, can result in false optimism that is counterproductive."[10]

Further support for this concept comes from the field of neuroscience. Emerging evidence indicates that a positive framework and feedback are essential to making changes. David Rock explains that "neurons literally need positive feedback to create new long-term connections."[11] It is through the formation of new long-term neural connections that individuals grow, learn, and develop.

Research at the intersection of mindfulness and neuroscience shows that a focus on observing positive qualities actually rewires your brain. For our own self-protection, the brain is "wired" to remember negative experiences and is "like Velcro for negative experiences but Teflon for positive ones."[12] What your mind focuses on and pays attention to over time will begin to shape your brain. Such neuroplasticity can lead to long-term change in rewiring your brain to perceive more positive experiences. "Over time, taking in the good could actually turn your brain's negativity bias into a responsivity bias—that will help you stay centered, strong, happy and healthy,"[13] explains Dr. Rick Hanson, author of *Hardwiring Happiness*. The Anytime Coaching practice of observing, especially focusing on positive qualities in yourself and your employees, will reshape neural connections to help you become more focused and resilient.

■ ■ ■ ■ ■ ■ **EXERCISE**
## Observing Positives

Read the following case study and respond to the questions that follow.

Keri is a recently promoted young supervisor in a small technical division within a larger organization. She was an outstanding analyst who worked quietly on her own without needing much supervision from her manager, Kevin. Since Keri was promoted to supervisor, her work style has changed dramatically. She constantly comes into Kevin's office and interrupts him with questions. The disruptions bother Kevin, so much so that he believes Keri is in over her head and thinks the promotion may have been a big mistake.

Questions:

If you were Kevin, what would you do in this situation?

_____

_____

What is positive about Keri coming to see Kevin frequently?

_____

_____

What are Keri's positive possibilities as a supervisor?

_____

_____

How could you use coaching to help encourage and motivate Keri as a new supervisor?

_____

_____

To improve his working relationship with Keri and support her, Kevin could observe Keri with a new set of eyes and see the positives in her behavior:

- She is enthusiastic about being a new supervisor, and her frequent interruptions signify her eagerness.
- She wants to do her job correctly, and asking so many questions helps her get the information she needs.

Historically, Keri has preferred to work quietly and alone; it is unlikely that she intends to interrupt Kevin's work indefinitely.

■ ■ ■ ■ ■ **PRACTICE TOOL**
Focusing on Positives

This tool is a simple reminder to pause before you engage with your employees. Remind yourself of their positive qualities or simply notice how you feel when an employee enters your office. It will take patience and practice, but by focusing on positives, you will create opportunities for Anytime Coaching.

When observing your employees, it is essential to appreciate what is already working for you and does not need to be solved or fixed. If you believe there are positive possibilities, you will see them.

## ■ ■ ■ Observing Nonverbal and Emotional Cues in Communication

The second technique in the practice of observing is noticing nonverbal and emotional cues in communication. There are three components of face-to-face communication, known as the three "V"s:

- Verbal (the words spoken)
- Vocal (the tone of voice)
- Visual (nonverbal expression, known as body language).

Many people assume that the verbal component is the most important aspect of face-to-face communication. But psychologist Albert Mehrabian overturned this assumption in *Silent Messages* in 1971.[14] Mehrabian's research found the following about face-to-face interpersonal exchanges:

- Words (verbal) account for only 7 percent of the message.
- Tone of voice accounts for 38 percent of the message.
- Body language (visual) accounts for 55 percent of the message.

The 7-38-55 Rule, which suggests that the meaning we derive from a speaker is most heavily influenced by his or her body language, is based on Mehrabian's research. It underscores how important it is to note nonverbal cues and tone in addition to someone's words.

■ ■ ■ ■ ■ ■ **PRINCIPLE**
> Anytime coaches pay close attention to all aspects of communication, including verbal (words), voice (tone), and visual (nonverbal).

How does the 7-38-55 Rule apply to the practice of observing? As an anytime coach, you should closely observe your employees' nonverbal communication during conversations. Look for facial expressions: Are their eyes open, bright, and making contact with yours—signs the person is engaged? Or are they looking away or down, which could be an indication that the person is uncomfortable or shy? Is the person smiling, suggesting he or she feels relaxed and happy? Or is he or she frowning, suggesting sadness or frustration?

### Other Uses of Nonverbal Communication

Nonverbal communication can indicate a change in your employee's workplace behavior or performance. For example, an employee who is normally talkative and involved in meetings may suddenly become quiet. The anytime coach observes this change in behavior and discusses it later with the employee during a coaching conversation, being sure to ask if the coach's observations are accurate and what the new behavior means.

Another seminal researcher of nonverbal communication, Dr. Paul Ekman, found that the six universal, cross-cultural facial expressions are anger, disgust, fear, happiness, sadness, and surprise. Even in the most diverse workplaces, Anytime Coaches recognize these emotions in relation to their employees' facial expressions.[15] We will explore how to ask questions regarding nonverbal communication and emotions in Chapter 3, The Practice of Inquiring.

"The body never lies."

—Martha Graham, American dancer and choreographer

## Nonverbal Cues and Their Significance

Here are some nonverbal cues and what they may mean:

| Nonverbal Cues | Possible Underlying Message |
|---|---|
| **Tone of Voice** | |
| Changes in pitch or tone | Nervous, excited |
| Loud tone or shouting | Angry, frustrated |
| Fast speed | Nervous, excited |
| Slow speed | Careful, calm, deliberate |
| **Eyes** | |
| Makes eye contact | Engaged, attentive |
| Avoids eye contact | Sad, nervous, distracted, disappointed |
| Quick eye movements | Worried, concerned, avoiding |
| Tears or watering eyes | Upset, sad |
| Furrowed eyebrows | Confused, uncertain |
| **Mouth** | |
| Smiling | Happy, relaxed, engaged |
| Frowning | Confused, angry, tense |
| Wide open | Surprised, alarmed |
| Biting lips | Nervous, tense |
| **Posture** | |
| Sitting upright, erect | Engaged, attentive to discussion |
| Slouching in chair | Disengaged, not interested |
| Arms crossed over chest | Defensive, bored, shut down |

According to the 7-38-55 Rule, tone of voice conveys 38 percent of the message in interpersonal communications, so it's important for anytime coaches to take note of the three elements of vocal tone:

- *Volume.* An employee prone to yelling conveys a nonverbal message of anger, frustration, or not feeling heard. An employee who speaks almost too softly to be heard may want to slip unnoticed into the background.

- *Speed of speech.* An employee who speaks rapidly may be excited or nervous; one who speaks slowly and deliberately may be cautious about what he or she is saying.
- *Pitch.* An employee with a flat monotone pitch may be feeling a lack of emotion or disengagement. Fluctuations to a higher or lower pitch may indicate excitement or a change in emotion.

---

■ ■ ■ ■ ■　**PRACTICE TOOL**
**Create a Nonverbal Communication Observation Log**

In a meeting at which you are free to observe other people, spend a few minutes observing two individuals' nonverbal communication, paying attention to body language and tone of voice; take mental notes on what you see.

**Body Language**

　Eyes (looking away or down from others, sad, tired, animated, alert, attentive)
　Hands (relaxed, tense, fidgety, animated, sweaty)
　Posture and body (erect, tense, relaxed, comfortable, slumped or hunched over, open stance)
　Arms (relaxed, crossed, defensive, waving or gesturing vigorously)
　Mouth (smiling, happy, tense, frowning, open)

**Tone of Voice**

　Volume of speech (soft, hard to hear, loud, shouting)
　Rate of speed (slow or fast)
　Pitch (fluctuating from high to low or monotone)

---

### The Concept of Congruence

Mehrabian's work also addresses the importance of congruence between voice, visual, and verbal messages.[16] In the practice of observing, you will notice congruence or lack of congruence between what people are saying (verbal), their tone (voice), and their nonverbal communication (visual). Congruence means the three Vs are in sync with each other. Anytime coaches pay very close attention to congruence or incongruence between words, tone of voice, and body language. They understand that people's true feelings are often not spoken in words but can be deciphered from nonverbal communication and vocal tone, especially when the words, voice, and body are not congruent. For example:

> *A manager is talking with his employee Jeff about an upcoming project with a very tight deadline. Jeff says, "I'm fine with the deadline and don't foresee any problems. I don't mind working all weekend." The manager observes that Jeff's voice is soft and he is speaking in a monotone. He sounds passive and withdrawn, not engaged and confident. The manager further notes that Jeff's head is down, and he is avoiding eye contact. Jeff's hands are clenched tightly and his posture is slumped, though he normally sits upright. The manager quickly observes the lack of congruence between Jeff's words, his tone of voice (passive, lacking engagement), and his body language (slumped, withdrawn, tense).*

Jeff may claim that he doesn't mind working over the weekend, but his body language sends a very different message. The slumped posture, clenched hands, and lack of eye contact indicate that he is *not* happy about the situation. As Mehrabian's work on congruence indicates, Jeff's body language communicates a more accurate message than do his words about how he feels and what he really wants to say.

Bear in mind that the culture and the country of origin of the person you are speaking with may affect his or her nonverbal communication style. Direct eye contact or active displays of emotion mean different things in different cultures and are not considered appropriate in all cultures. If you manage a diverse, multicultural workforce, we recommend you learn more about specific norms governing nonverbal communication that apply to your employees' cultures or countries of origin. Understanding cross-cultural differences in nonverbal communication will help you in your role as a manager as well as an anytime coach.[17]

■ ■ ■ ■ ■   **PRACTICE TOOL**
Checking Your Nonverbal Communication

The 7-38-55 Rule tells us that nonverbal cues play a critical role when you communicate with others. For this practice, you will do a quick check of your own nonverbal cues during coaching conversations with employees. You can begin to observe yourself as soon as an employee comes into your office. The following checklist is useful for this practice:

✓ *Body:* Are you sitting up straight and comfortably in your chair? Does your body language indicate that you're paying attention to the other person?
✓ *Hands:* Are your hands folded and natural or fidgety?
✓ *Face:* Is your mouth neutral? Smiling? Tense or frowning? Are your eyes looking at the other person?
✓ *Head:* Are you nodding your head in agreement as the person speaks, keeping your head down, or looking away?
✓ *Vocal tone:* Is your tone of voice appropriate? Too loud or soft? Fast or slow? Are you speaking in a monotone or using higher and lower tones for emphasis?

■ ■ ■ ■ ■ ■   **PRINCIPLE**

Anytime coaches observe the congruence or disparity in verbal and nonverbal communication with their employees.

■ ■ ■ ■ ■   **EXERCISE**
Nonverbal Communication and Emotions

List the nonverbal communication signals, including tone of voice and body language, you might expect from an employee who is experiencing each of the listed emotions.

| If an employee feels... | Tone of voice cues | Body language cues |
| --- | --- | --- |
| *Example: Excited about a task* | *high, talking fast* | *active hands, energetic* |
| Nervous about the manager's reaction | | |
| Frustrated at someone | | |
| Sad about a performance result | | |
| Confused about what to do next | | |
| Angry about being interrupted at a meeting | | |
| Afraid to make a mistake | | |
| Happy to see fellow team members | | |
| Passionate about the unit's mission | | |

---

**The Key to Nonverbal Observation**

As anytime coaches pay closer attention to nonverbal communication during conversations with others, they learn that a successful observer is a *nonjudgmental* observer. Nonjudgmental observation, a key aspect of mindfulness, requires you to simply observe without judging yourself or the other person. Watch your employees' nonverbal communication, but do not judge whether it is wrong or right or try to correct it.

Let's say you are discussing a deadline with one of your employees, and you notice that she is frowning. You may want to tell the employee to stop frowning, but that is judgmental observation. Instead, realize that her frown may indicate that she is concerned or confused. You can talk with her about your observations of nonverbal communication during a coaching conversation after you have learned more about Anytime Coaching and the practices of inquiring, listening, and responding.

---

## ▪ ▪ ▪ Self-Observation

An additional technique in the practice of observing is to observe yourself as a manager and anytime coach. You will need to become a better observer of your own management behavior as well as your own nonverbal communication. Doing so is an important skill and represents a big step forward toward becoming an effective anytime coach. The mindfulness excercises at the end of this chapter will enhance your self-awareness during the inevitable stresses of working with others.

### ▪ ▪ Observing Your Impulse to Direct: The Fast Results Gene

It is hard enough to find time to observe employees in the workplace; making time to reflect on your own interactions with others can be even more difficult. Why? The main culprit is an innate trait many managers have, which we call the fast results gene, or FRG.

The FRG enables you to stay highly motivated and to achieve results quickly. If you have the FRG, you will often use words such as "speed" and "results," and your body language will be active, especially during crunch periods and crisis situations when adrenaline is flowing and you are under pressure to finish your work.

How does the FRG shape your management and leadership style? If you have the FRG, you prize getting things done quickly, so you may be a highly directive manager: You tell your employees what to do, when to do it, and how to do it correctly and quickly.

There are certain management and workplace situations, such as emergencies or other urgent circumstances, in which it is vital to have a directive management style. Anytime Coaching, however, thrives on self-observation and understanding, which enable you to move beyond being a directive manager. Coaching means learning to resist the temptation of always telling people what to do.

■ ■ ■ ■ ■ ■ **PRINCIPLE**

> To resist the temptation to tell your employees what to do during coaching, you must tame your fast results gene (FRG).

In addition to having a positive impact in employee coaching conversations, learning to tame the FRG allows you to access your brain's higher level cortical system, which has positive implications for your sense of composure, thinking , and well-being. Remember, you have two brain systems that are in constant competition for your focus and attention: the higher, more rational, calmer but slower prefrontal cortex and the faster, reactive, negative-biased, emotionally based limbic system. Taming the FRG will subdue the fiery limbic system, including the powerful neurochemical cortisol associated with stress, which is known to lead to cognitive, emotional, and physical fatigue. When the FRG is running at full speed during a crisis or panic, fear kicks in and cortisol flows.

Dr. Edward M. Hallowell explains the physiology of the FRG this way:

> *Fear shifts us into survival mode and thus prevents fluid learning and nuanced understanding.... When the frontal lobes approach capacity and we begin to fear that we can't keep up, the relationship between the higher and lower regions of the brain takes an ominous turn. In response to what is going on the brain, the rest of the body has shifted into crisis mode and changed its baseline physiology from peace and quiet to red alert.*[18]

When you face a workplace challenge, the FRG will urge you to direct, react, and move to immediate problem solving in the face of time pressures. But this is not always the best approach or solution. The practice of observing and taming the FRG quiets this innate, loud impulse and allows you to access a calmer, more appropriate response.

Taming the FRG is an important technique to add to your management toolbox. After Gary D. Leclair, a prominent attorney and co-founder/chairman of a national law firm, learned the Anytime Coaching approach, he shared why it is essential to tame the FRG: "I have relied on and benefited from my FRG for many years—as a former competitive athlete and attorney. The FRG can be a great strength like a hammer. But you don't use a hammer all the time." He learned not to rely solely on his FRG when he became an anytime coach, and he gained new tools to help him work with other partners in the firm.

When you practice self-observation, you will begin to notice the FRG impulse to use a traditional command-and-control management style with employees. You will start to see yourself rushing to get results, rather than slowing down to talk to employees, and feeling impatient during conversations.

### Taming the FRG

Anytime coaches understand that to develop, motivate, and engage people, you must first observe and then tame the FRG. This means not telling others what to do unless it is truly necessary to do so. Curbing your FRG impulses will give you more time to pay attention to your employees and to notice what is going on around you. By observing and curbing your own FRG, you take another step toward becoming an anytime coach.

---

**STORY**
**Tom Tames the FRG**

It was Thursday at 2:00 p.m., and Tom, a busy executive, was facing a 5:00 p.m. deadline to complete an important PowerPoint® presentation for the senior executive of the division. Tom's natural preference is to involve himself heavily in projects, but he has been working hard on changing his leadership style from "command and control" to visionary and inspirational—and has tried to tame his FRG.

Under pressure to finish the presentation, Tom recalls, "All I wanted to do was tell my staff exactly what to do. It was efficient and was definitely more comfortable for me." But Tom recognized that he needed to change his approach. "In the past, I would have jumped in, but I decided to step back and change how I observed this situation. I realized the two managers working on the presentation were very competent. The managers were motivated to get the presentation done correctly, and the staff felt the same time pressure."

So Tom just asked a few questions to ensure the analysis was complete and offered to help at any time before the deadline. Tom explains: "Because I changed my perspective on the situation, I was comfortable with the staff finalizing the presentation at 4:15, which would give me 45 minutes to review it. I did not jump in at 2:00 and bark out the format for the charts and design because I felt nervous—which was my old style. As a coach, I told my employees to think about the senior executive's perspective while working on the slides."

Tom's staff came through, and the presentation was a success for the senior executive. "The staff did a better job in parts of the presentation than I would have," Tom says. "I am glad I could shut down my FRG and let my employees do the job they were asked to complete."

The field of neuroscience also helps explain why taming the impulse to tell others what to do is an important step toward better people management. David Rock writes: "Our standard practices for improving performance involve techniques that are largely ineffective at helping others: giving advice, solving problems or trying to work out how people need to think. To maximize our effectiveness as leaders, it is time to give up second guessing what people's brains need and become masters of helping others think for themselves."[19]

The directive leadership style your FRG demands could prevent your employees and associates from thinking creatively, resolving their own workplace problems, and having critical "aha" moments necessary for their professional development. Curbing your FRG impulses will help you notice opportunities for coaching, which takes time and patience but ultimately allows employees to take on more responsibility and improve their performance.

### PRINCIPLE

Anytime coaches remember that recent findings in neuroscience support coaching practices that help others "rewire" their brains for new actions and results.

■ ■ ■ ■ ■  **PRACTICE TOOL**
Noticing Your FRG throughout the Day

The following questions will expand your awareness of—and help you say no to—your FRG.

What triggers your FRG, and how can you tell when it wants to take over?

Do you sense your FRG at a certain time of day? When you are looking at your email inbox? Skipping lunch? Running late to a meeting?

*Note any specific triggers that make you feel rushed and less likely to coach others.*

Does it feel easier and faster to tell people what to do? Are you feeling rushed to complete work?

*Remind yourself the FRG has kicked in and that Anytime Coaching tames the FRG. Repeat this to yourself during the day.*

Do you believe that your employees do not work as quickly as you do?

*Remind yourself that they work differently than you do, and that is okay.*

When you feel the FRG taking over, how do you calm yourself down?

*Think about what helps you feel less urgency. Take a short break to refocus and redirect yourself toward an Anytime Coaching mindset. Try taking a few deep breaths or following the two-minute breathing sequence outlined at the end of this chapter. Stand up and stretch your legs. Take a short walk around the office. Go get a glass of water or a healthy snack.*

■ ■ ■ ■ ■ ■ ■ ■ ■

"What is necessary to change a person is to change his awareness of himself."

—ABRAHAM MASLOW, AMERICAN PSYCHOLOGIST

■ ■ ■ ■ ■ ■ ■ ■ ■

## ■ ■ ■  Observing Your Mindful Presence

The concept of mindfulness has tremendous applicability to the practice of observing and will also enhance all the other practices of Anytime Coaching. We have created a simple approach we are calling PAF: being more *present*, more *aware*, and more *focused*.

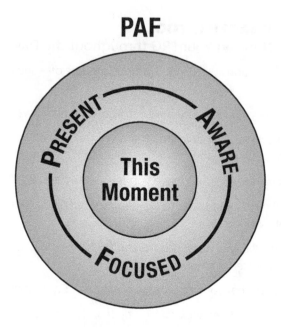

*Present.* Think only of this moment, in this place, and nothing else. Develop a habit of allowing distracting thoughts to just slip away while you keep your attention on the present.

*Aware.* Be conscious of what your senses are telling you: what your eyes are seeing, what your ears are hearing , and what your body is experiencing. Again, allow random thoughts about a work issue, a difficult conversation, or a deadline to pass on by. Simply return your attention to noticing what is happening in this moment.

*Focused.* During a mindfulness practice, the most common focus is your breath, something that is always there and is easy to return to when other thoughts intrude and then fade away. When you are in the middle of a workday, focus can refer to what's most important—in this conversation, in this situation, with this person—right now.

### ▧  Using PAF to Improve the Practice of Observation

Being less reactive and more resilient enables you to be more deliberate in observing yourself and others and to make more intentional choices in the words you speak and the actions you take. Mary VandeVanter, an expert in mindfulness, explains:

> *What we know about the human brain is that we tend to be on autopilot much of the time, going about our lives but being somewhere else. Never really being completely here. People who actively practice mindfulness report that they are far more present in their lives. Mindfulness also seems to really impact the quality and depth of their work. They are much less likely to make impulsive decisions. Because they are more available to themselves, their decisions seem to come from a place of deeper stability and creativity. Mindfulness also appears to help people take more responsibility for their own behavior, to be less reactive to the behavior of others, and to have more realistic expectations of life in general.*[20]

Another outcome of observing yourself and others is an enhanced ability to pay more attention to other people's body language and the congruence between what they say, how they say it, and what they do with their face and body. Those in your presence who sense you are focused on your conversation will also be positively affected by your concentrated attention. Without saying a word, you are conveying that the person matters to you; most people will appreciate knowing and feeling this sense of your interested presence.

Finally, when you are in a centered frame of mind, it is more likely that your own words, voice, and physical cues will line up and appear congruent to those around you, sending the message that what you are saying is an authentic representation of what you are thinking and feeling.

As explained by Rebecca Zafir in *The Zen of Listening*:

> *What exactly happens in our bodies during meditation that allows us to calm down and focus? One theory is that meditation lowers the body's responsiveness to the stress hormone norepinephrine. This theory is attributed to Robert Benson, M.D., president of the Mind/ Body Medical Institute at Deaconess Hospital in Boston, Massachusetts, and author of* The Relaxation Response. *In one study, subjects were presented with a stressful situation while their heart rate and blood pressure were monitored. Subjects who had meditated twice a day for a month did not experience a rise in heart rate and blood pressure despite a rise in norepinephrine. Subjects who had not meditated experienced the usual increased blood pressure and heart rate. Many programs designed to help people with weight control, coronary heart disease, smoking cessation, and depression now encourage meditation as part of the treatment protocol.*[21]

## ■ ■ ■ ■ ■ ■ **PRINCIPLE**

Anytime coaches strive to be more present, focused, and aware when interacting with others in order to get better results.

### ■ ■ Learning to be Mindful

The following exercises can serve as starting points for experiencing mindful observation. Begin with one that looks easy for you and fits into your workday. Spending even one or two minutes practicing mindfulness will be beneficial. Don't worry or feel overwhelmed if mindfulness seems foreign and challenging. Even skeptics have found that the repeated practice of stopping, focusing on the breath, and letting intruding thoughts drift away will, over time, enable a calmer, more deliberate approach to everyday dilemmas. Remember that while a brief mindfulness break has the appearance of just sitting still and being unengaged in work, your brain and body are actually doing essential "work" that has long-term rewards.[22]

■ ■ ■ ■ ■   **PRACTICE TOOL**
### Taking Two Quiet Minutes

The practice of self-observation starts at the beginning of the day, when you first get into your office. Before you turn on the computer or start to work, take two minutes to sit quietly in a chair, close your eyes, and notice how you feel. What kind of mood are you in? Are you ready to look for opportunities for Anytime Coaching? Are you already feeling rushed even though the day has not yet begun?

If your mind is racing, your FRG is active. To create calm and tame the FRG, focus on breathing for two minutes. Try the following short breathing sequence to engage your mind and body.

- Close your eyes.
- Notice how you are sitting. Is your back straight? Are your feet on the floor and grounded? Sit up straight but comfortably. Rest your hands on your lap.
- Inhale and exhale deeply three to five times to begin your breathing sequence.
- Count the length of each inhalation and exhalation. Is the inhalation longer than the exhalation?
- Make your exhalations longer than your inhalations. Repeat this for five breaths.
- Put both your hands on your belly.
- As you breathe in, imagine that you are sending your breath to your belly. Envision your belly as a balloon. With each inhale, push out the balloon and make it expand. As you exhale, the balloon will shrink and your hands will sink in. Repeat this balloon-belly breathing for five to ten breaths.
- Return to normal breathing for three or more breaths, but still maintain focus on your breath only.
- Open your eyes. Does your FRG feel calmer and your mind less agitated?

■ ■ ■ ■ ■    **PRACTICE TOOL**
Mindfulness on the Move

Some of us are by nature more active than others, and the idea of sitting still "doing nothing" may sound difficult—or just a waste of time. An alternative approach is to stay mindful while "on the move."[23]

For example, let's suppose you have a meeting in ten minutes in a conference room on another floor of your building. Prepare your materials in advance. Then use the ten minutes to follow a route to the meeting that involves more walking than usual. While taking that walk, maintain a viewpoint that you will "just notice" what passes by—the color of the walls and ceiling, the temperature and whether it changes from one floor to another—all the while paying attention to the evenness of your footsteps and the rhythm of your breathing.

When you engage in "mindfulness on the move," what is *not* happening is ruminating about the troublesome colleague you are about to meet, the agenda you think is incomplete, or your worries about whether your ideas will be heard. You will arrive at the meeting in a frame of mind that is calmer and more focused on the moment, making it easier for you to maintain that presence throughout the meeting.

■ ■ **Practicing Mindfulness throughout Your Day**

As you go through your day, from house to car, from car to office, from meeting to meeting, continue to be present with just the sights, sounds, and sensations right in front of you. Notice how the lighting and temperature change from the parking garage to the elevator; the textures of walls, carpeting, and ceilings; the sounds of your footsteps; your breathing; and how you suddenly come upon a colleague in the hallway who wants to have a conversation. Make these observations with no judgment at all—only noticing.

Should judgmental or critical phrases enter your mind, let them pass by and maintain a serene sense that this is the only moment there is. If you have only a minute to chat on the way to your meeting, then—with full congruence of words, tone, and body—gently tell your colleague you are on your way to a meeting and you will call later.

Here's an image to help you picture what ongoing mindfulness looks like: Think of a continuous line with just occasional small waves on it, and then think of that line as your "calm meter." This imaginary line shows your overall demeanor with no spikes of emotion, dips of anxiety, blips of uncertainty, or loops of ungrounded judgments and interpretations. This imaginary, relatively straight line symbolizes when you are your most calm and present self throughout the day, demonstrating quiet certainty and solidity—a presence readily discernible to others. People around you will sense your centeredness and your attentive presence, and they will be drawn to it.

YOU: When you are present, aware, and focused

YOU: When you are *not* present, aware, and focused.

This example of "mindfulness in the moment" is representative of a type of mini meditation that is possible throughout the workday. Mini meditation may seem frivolous or just too hard to do in the face of all the pressures, deadlines, and competing commitments in an average workday. Developing a regular practice of longer, more sustained mindfulness exercise will help condition the brain to enter shorter meditations more easily. [24]

■ ■ ■ ■ ■   **PRACTICE TOOL**
**Focus on the Moment**

While driving to work, you can maintain your alertness to the safety concerns and the mechanics of driving while taking in what your senses bring you. Notice how smooth or bumpy the pavement is, the rhythm of the windshield wipers if it is raining, the changing light patterns if you are commuting early in the morning or late at night, the texture of the steering wheel in your hands, and the feel of the air conditioning or heat in your car.

From time to time, you might decide to eat lunch by yourself. Whether you bring your lunch, buy carry-out, or go to a restaurant, take your meal to a quiet place without your cellphone and where people will not distract you. If you are having lunch outdoors, pay attention to the sounds around you: traffic, rustling leaves, birds, airplanes overhead. If you have found an empty conference room, note what is happening outside the window, or simply observe the quiet of an empty room. In only a few minutes, you will begin to tame the FRG, reduce cortisol, and calm your nerves; you will be practicing mindfulness.

These experiences of "focusing on the moment" will give you practice at directing your attention, calming your mind, and letting intruding thoughts pass by and fade away. Just as with the exercise machines at a health club, repetition builds both habit and strength. All will lead you to be more present, more aware, and more focused throughout the day. Repeating such practices will make focusing on the moment a habit that will grow stronger with time.

As you move along the road of Anytime Coaching to the next practice, inquiring, remember to focus on creating positive possibilities, noticing nonverbal cues, observing congruence and incongruence in communication, and taming your FRG. Look for opportunities to practice observing the present, creating mindfulness moments that support the grounded self. As you practice, you will improve your Anytime Coaching skills, which will enhance your interactions with employees and improve their day-to-day performance.

### NOTES

1   Brigid Shulte, *Overworked: Work, Love and Play When No One Has the Time* (New York: Farrar, Strauss and Giroux, 2014), p. 57.

2   Robert Cooper, *Get Out of Your Own Way* (New York: Crown Business Press, 2006), p. 25.

3  Daniel Goleman, *Focus: The Hidden Driver of Excellence* (New York: HarperCollins, 2013), p. 171.

4  Ibid.

5  Research on the impact of positive emotions includes diverse fields such as neuroscience, neuropsychology, positive psychology, stress management, and organizational development. Among the best known academic researchers in the field are Barbara Frederickson (University of North Carolina), Richard Boyatzis (Case Western Reserve), Martin Seligman (University of Pennsylvania), Joseph LeDoux (New York University), Matthew Lieberman (UCLA), Ellen Langer (Harvard), and David Cooperrider (Case Western Reserve).

6  Rick Hanson, *Hardwiring Happiness: The New Brain Science of Contentment, Calm and Happiness* (New York: Penguin Random House, 2013), p.75.

7  David Cooperrider, *Appreciative Inquiry: Rethinking Human Organization Toward a Positive Theory of Change* (Champaign, IL: Stipes Publishing, 2000), p. 5.

8  Ibid.

9  Tom Rath and Donald Clifton, *How Full Is Your Bucket?* (New York: Gallup Press, 2004), p. 55.

10 Ibid., p. 57.

11 David Rock, *Quiet Leadership* (New York: Collins Business, 2006), p. 25.

12 Rick Hanson, *Hardwiring Happiness: The New Brain Science of Contentment, Calm and Happiness* (New York: Penguin Random House, 2013), p. 75.

13 Ibid., p. 52.

14 Albert Mehrabian, *Silent Messages: Implicit Communication and Emotions and Attitudes* (Belmont, CA: Wadsworth, 1971), pp. 43–44.

15 Paul Ekman, *Emotions Revealed, Second Edition: Recognizing Faces and Feelings to Improve Communication and Emotional Life* (New York: Henry Holt, 2007), p. 10.

16 Albert Mehrabian, *Silent Messages: Implicit Communication and Emotions and Attitudes* (Belmont, CA: Wadsworth, 1971), pp. 43–44.

17 Regarding the importance of understanding cultural differences in communication styles and diversity in the workplace, we recommend the well-established work of Loden and Rosener or Gardenswartz and Rowe (see Recommended Reading).

18 Dr. Edward Hallowell, "Overloaded Circuits," *Harvard Business Review*, January 2005, p. 4.

19 David Rock, *Quiet Leadership* (New York: Collins Business, 2006), p. 27.

20 Mary VandeVanter, LCSW, is a psychotherapist and workplace trauma consultant in private practice in Alexandria, Virginia. She teaches weekly mindfulness meditation classes and is an instructor of the

Mindfulness Based Stress Reduction method pioneered in the late 1970s by Jon Kabat-Zinn at the University of Massachusetts Medical Center.

21 Rebecca Z. Shafir, *The Zen of Listening* (Wheaton, IL: Quest Books, 2000), p. 242.

22 In Jon Kabat-Zinn's *Full Catastrophe Living* (New York: Bantam, 2013), p. xli, we learn that "eight weeks of Mindfulness Based Stress Reduction training leads to thickening of a number of different regions of the brain associated with learning and memory, emotion regulation, the sense of self, and perspective taking."

23 For more on meditation practices for the active person, read *Mindfulness to Go: How to Meditate While You're On the Move* by David Harp (see Recommended Reading). The mini meditation described was inspired by Harp's approach.

24 To explore developing a sustained practice of longer, more focused meditations, we recommend *Finding the Space to Lead: A Practical Guide to Mindful Leadership* by Janice Marturano (see Recommended Reading). She describes and recommends a number of specific meditations for leaders in the workplace.

## RECOMMENDED READING

Baker, Dan, and Cameron Stauth. *What Happy People Know*. New York: St. Martin's Griffin, 2003.

Brach, Tara. *Mindfulness Meditation: Nine Guided Practices to Awaken Presence and Open Your Heart*. Audiobook. Sounds True, 2012.

Cooperrider, David, Peter F. Sorensen, Diana Whitney, and Therese F. Yaeger, eds. *Appreciative Inquiry: Rethinking Human Organization Toward a Positive Theory of Change*. Champaign, IL: Stipes Publishing, 2000.

Gardenswartz, Lee, and Anita Rowe. *Diverse Teams at Work: Capitalizing on the Power of Diversity*. New York: McGraw Hill, 1994.

Harp, David. *Mindfulness to Go: How to Meditate While You're On the Move*. Oakland, CA: New Harbinger Publications, 2011.

Kabat-Zinn, Jon. *Mindfulness for Beginners*. Boulder, CO: Sounds True, 2012.

Loden, Marilyn, and Judy B. Rosener. *Workforce America!: Managing Employee Diversity as a Vital Resource*. Chicago: Irwin Professional Publishing, 1991.

Marturano, Janice. *Finding the Space to Lead: A Practical Guide to Mindful Leadership*. NY: Bloomsbury Press, 2014.

Medina, John. *Brain Rules*. Seattle: Pear Press, 2008.

Mehrabian, Albert. *Silent Messages: Implicit Communication and Emotions and Attitudes*. Belmont, CA: Wadsworth, 1971.

Navarro, Joe. *What Every Body Is Saying*. New York: William Morrow/ Harper Collins Publishers, 2008.

Rath, Tom, and Donald Clifton. *How Full Is Your Bucket?* New York: Gallup Press, 2004.

Rock, David. *Quiet Leadership*. New York: Collins Business, 2006.

Seligman, Martin. *Authentic Happiness: Using the New Positive Psychology to Realize Your Potential for Lasting Fulfillment*. New York: Free Press, 2002.

Shafir, Rebecca Z. *The Zen of Listening*. Wheaton, IL: Quest Books, 2000.

Thornton, Mark. *Meditation in a New York Minute: Super Calm for the Super Busy*. Boulder, CO: Sounds True, 2004.

# 3 The Practice of Inquiring

"Judge others by their questions rather than by their answers."

—Voltaire, 18th century French Enlightenment writer

The practice of inquiring provides tools, a structure, and discipline for asking powerful and insightful questions in your coaching. Anytime coaches recognize that these kinds of questions often lead to important conversations with employees; the practice of inquiring will encourage employees to communicate more openly with you. In fact, the practice of inquiring is at the very heart of Anytime Coaching. All the practices matter, but you cannot coach without inquiring.

■ ■ ■ ■ ■ ■  **PRINCIPLE**

Anytime coaches recognize that questions are the doorway to meaningful conversations with employees.

Inquiring offers many benefits. Effective questions are essential tools that help those you coach think differently—more critically, creatively, and strategically. Good questions help others open up new mental pathways as they clarify problems and tasks, help make decisions, implement new solutions, and learn from performance gains. Improved employee performance is the ultimate aim of Anytime Coaching.

Asking powerful questions benefits not only the employee, but also you. "Questions help the questioner find a better understanding of themselves, comprehend more clearly why they do the things they do and clarify their thinking,"[1] explains author Michael Marquardt. You learn about yourself through the act of questioning. You will also come to understand more about your employees' work, interests, and motives, building mutual trust and enhancing your working relationships. Through the practice of inquiring, your own and your employees' knowledge and insight will grow.

The practice of inquiring is linked to the other parts of the Anytime Coaching model. Questions are key components of the practices of observing and responding; they must follow observing and precede responding. Questions also tame your FRG's impulse to direct and respond, helping you focus and communicate with others by asking questions and learning their perspectives. Inquiring connects the other practices.

In this chapter, we provide diagnostic tools to help you first determine the purpose of your questions and then choose the types of questions that will maximize learning and communication. We also help you take a closer look at employees' personalities and work habits, choose the appropriate timing and location for Anytime Coaching, and overcome two big misconceptions that often limit coaching opportunities.

## ▣ ▣ ▣ **The Power of Questions**

The chart below highlights what questions can do and why they are important in Anytime Coaching.

| What questions can do | Why this is important |
|---|---|
| Help people think differently | Employees gain competence in thinking and solving problems in new ways |
| Build greater trust | People become more comfortable opening up and speaking freely about what is really important |
| Begin or enhance relationships | Employees create stronger working and personal ties to others and the workplace |
| Help you understand your employees' views and positions | Employees are able to explain and share their viewpoints, which may lead to alternative solutions |
| Clarify a problem or task | Employees are better able to identify and solve problems and thereby achieve results |
| Create new solutions | Employees may find faster, more cost-effective, and sustainable ways to resolve issues |
| Prompt learning and growth | Employees increase their knowledge and self-awareness, enabling better performance |

Think about a time someone asked you a powerful question that affected your work or life. Powerful questions are "provocative queries that put a halt to evasion and confusion. By asking a powerful question, [you] invite clarity, action, and discovery at a whole new level."[2] Such questions have the ability to elicit our most important thoughts and feelings, and they can lead to action. As an anytime coach, take a few moments to reflect on the following powerful questions:

- ▪ What is really important to you?
- ▪ What do you consider success for you at work? In life?
- ▪ What part of your work do you enjoy the most? Why?

▪ How does your work as an anytime coach make a difference to others?

▪ When are you at your best?

What did you notice or learn from these questions? The practice of inquiring enables you to ask your employees simple yet deeply engaging questions. You may be the first person to ask your employees powerful questions, and your questions could have a meaningful and lasting effect on them.

To be sure that your powerful questions do not come across as an interrogation, maintain your mindful focus on the overall tone of the conversation when you ask the questions. By being rooted in the present, you are intentionally being supportive and helpful. Observe the pauses between your own and your employee's comments, questions, and responses; there's no need to rush. Maintaining an interested yet unhurried stance, asking powerful questions with a mindful presence that telegraphs your genuine interest in your employee's replies. By regularly practicing mindfulness, you will develop a calm and clear mind that can more easily focus on the questions that are most appropriate to the situation.

Asking powerful questions is one of a manager's most important tools. What happens in the brain when a powerful question is posed? When we ask the right questions, people reflect and their brains go into the alpha state. "Alpha waves have been found to correlate with the release of the neurotransmitter serotonin, a chemical messenger that increases relaxation and eases pain. So when we reflect, we tend to feel good."[3] As anytime coaches, when we ask our employees powerful questions, at the right time, they not only feel good but can experience insights and new awareness.

■ ■ ■ ■ ■ ■ ■ ■ ■

"Sometimes questions are more important than answers."

—NANCY WILLARD, AUTHOR AND POET

■ ■ ■ ■ ■ ■ ■ ■ ■ ■

Practical tools and techniques to help you implement the practice of inquiring include the following:

- Analyzing the three purposes of questions
- Understanding the four types of questions
- Matching the purpose and type of questions
- Considering the receiver of questions
- Choosing the right time to inquire.
- Choosing the right place to coach.

### Analyzing the Three Purposes of Questions

The first technique is to clarify the purpose of your questions before asking them. The practice of inquiring involves three categories of questions, based on their purpose:

- Questions seeking information
- Questions involving relationships
- Questions about solutions.

*Questions Seeking Information*

When you need facts, you ask questions seeking information. These questions are most helpful when you need more information to better understand a situation or problem. They are also helpful when someone has offered you an opinion but not many facts. For example, when an employee says, "That meeting was interesting," you can probe for greater understanding by simply asking for some facts: "What did you discuss there?" "What was on the agenda?" "Who was there?"

The following are other examples of questions seeking information:

**Why did you agree with the team's decision to change the operations workflow?**

**Benefit**: Identifying the pros and cons of a decision helps the employee process and further understand his or her own thinking.

**How did you calculate the net loss ratio on the spreadsheet?**

**Benefit:** You will learn more about how the employee came to a decision and what information was used. In cases where excellent judgment was used, you can recognize and compliment the employee. Where there was a mistake or problem, you can surface the issue through inquiring in an effort to help the employee learn and improve performance.

### Questions Involving Relationships

When you need to develop your employees' commitment, build trust, or enhance relationships, you ask questions involving relationships. These questions engage your employees in powerful conversations about what is important to them and deepen your relationship with them. Some examples: "What is concerning you?" "Why is this important to you?" "What can I do to help you?"

Here are other examples of questions involving relationships:

**What parts of your job do you like and dislike the most?**

**Benefit:** You can engage employees by asking about their likes and dislikes, strengths and weaknesses. Your questions show that you care about the them.

You gave a terrific report last week to the regional director. What is in this week's report that will ensure that it is as strong as the previous report?

**Benefit:** This question builds the employee's confidence and thus strengthens your relationship.

### Questions about Solutions

When you need to focus on getting and sustaining tangible results or need to foster change, you ask questions about solutions. These questions generate new problem-solving opportunities within the workplace. They also help stimulate creativity and learning. Examples include: "How could that be done in a different way?" "What is your best thinking right now on the topic?" "What other options are available?" "What hasn't been tried in the past?"

Here are some more questions about solutions:

**How should we prioritize the team's action-item list?**

**Benefit**: This question helps the employee figure out the best way to accomplish something, allowing him or her to learn what is likely to work best and what might be ineffective.

**What do you think would be the best way to handle the conflict over reporting assignments between HQ and the field?**

**Benefit:** This question also helps the employee think through solutions, coming up with a conclusion and the reasoning that led to that conclusion.

Now that you know how important it is to understand the purpose of your questions, let's take a look at what can happen when this principle is forgotten and a manager does not match a question to the purpose.

When Tom, a senior manager, asks his employee, Sarah, "How do you feel about the project?" Sarah responds, "I feel really good about it. I am excited to be on the team." If Tom were trying to understand Sarah's feelings and enhance his relationship with her, this would be an appropriate question. But in this scenario Tom wants to clarify the project status; his purpose is to gain information. So Tom has asked the wrong question. A stronger information-seeking question would be, "Sarah, what is going well with the project?" Then he might ask, "What challenges are there with the project?"

■ ■ ■ ■ ■ ■ ■ ■ ■ ■

"Good questions outrank easy answers."

—PAUL SAMUELSON, AMERICAN NEOCLASSICAL ECONOMIST AND NOBEL

PRIZE WINNER

---

### Seven Words to Memorize

To help you determine the purpose of a question, we recommend you memorize the following seven words: "What is the purpose of my question?" Instead of asking the first question that comes to mind, take a few seconds to repeat these seven words to yourself. Once you have answered your own question, then query your employee. These seven words will help you ask more meaningful and powerful questions that will meet your needs and help your employees. You will be more likely to ask the right question at the right time to the right employee.

■ ■ ■ ■ ■ **PRACTICE TOOL**
The Purpose of Questions

Think of an important Anytime Coaching conversation you would like to have with an employee in the next week.

Name of employee: _____

Describe the issue you'd like to address with the employee.

_____

_____

What are the top three questions you would like to ask your employee? Circle the purpose of each question.

1. _____(information, relationship, solution)

2. _____(information, relationship, solution)

3. _____(information, relationship, solution)

Write additional questions to address your intended purpose.

1. _____

2. _____

3. _____

## Understanding the Four Types of Questions

In addition to distinguishing between the purposes of questions, anytime coaches also differentiate between four types of questions. This is important to the practice of inquiring because it gives you the opportunity to select the most useful and powerful questions in Anytime Coaching.

The four types of questions are:

■ Closed-ended questions
■ Open-ended questions
■ Questions seeking opinions
■ Questions addressing emotions and nonverbal communication.

## Closed-ended Questions

When you need simple, one-word answers such as "yes" or "no," or a specific fact or piece of data and not much detail, you ask closed-ended questions.

Here are examples of closed-ended questions:

- Did you send the email to the division director? (answer: yes)
- What dollar amount did you use in the estimate? (answer: $1.25)
- How many staff people are impacted by the reorganization? (answer: 24)
- Do you prefer option 1 or option 2? (answer: option 2)

Notice how little information is exchanged between the employee and the anytime coach. Closed-ended questions are often used to focus on facts (what, where, how) or to find out if the receiver agrees with a statement. Plus, closed-ended questions are helpful if the receiver often rambles.

## Open-ended Questions

When you need an employee to open up and share more information, you ask open-ended questions. Open-ended questions often begin with "what," "how," or "why." They help anytime coaches learn more about an employee because they do not elicit simple one-word answers but instead encourage the employee to share his or her ideas and create an atmosphere of greater trust and rapport in the workplace. Anytime coaches rely heavily on open-ended questions for more powerful conversations.

```
┌─────────────────────────────────────────────────────────────────────┐
│ Anytime Coaching Question Stems                                       │
│ What more can you tell me about. . . . . . . . . . . . . . . . . . . . . . . . . . .? │
│ What do you really want to happen with . . . . . . . . . . . . . . . . . . . . .? │
│ What is important to you about . . . . . . . . . . . . . . . . . . . . . . and why? │
│ What would success regarding . . . . . . . . . . . . . . . . . . look like to you? │
│ What other options can you think of regarding. . . . . . . . . . . . . . . . .? │
│ What do you think is happening with . . . . . . . . . . . . . . . . . . . . . . .? │
│ What matters to you most regarding. . . . . . . . . . . . . . . . . . . . . . . .? │
│ What are you experiencing and learning in . . . . . . . . . . . . . . . . . . .? │
│ How do you see . . . . . . . . . . . . . . . . . . . . . . . . . . . . . . . . . . . .? │
│ How does this impact . . . . . . . . . . . . . . . . . . . . . . . . . . . . . . . .? │
│ How can I help you succeed at . . . . . . . . . . . . . . . . . . . . . . . . . . .? │
│ How do you define success with. . . . . . . . . . . . . . . . . . . . . . . . . .? │
└─────────────────────────────────────────────────────────────────────┘
```

These are some examples of open-ended questions:

**What did you focus on in your email to the division director?**

**Answer:** "I wrote about the regulatory change and its impact on our division in terms of personnel, policies, and procedures." The answer helps the manager understand the content of the email.

**Why did you select that dollar amount for the estimate?**

**Answer:** "I used $1.25 because the figure reflects the recently published adjusted rate of inflation." The answer helps the manager understand the employee's rationale.

**What concerns do you have about how the reorganization will affect the staff?**

**Answer:** "I am really concerned about the morale of the 25 employees in our division, and I don't know who they will report to now."

The answer demonstrates the employee's interest and attention to the team.

**Why do you prefer option 1 or option 2?**

**Answer:** "Option 2 is the stronger of the two because it has defined performance-management criteria. I think this makes our progress more measurable." The answer shows the employee's analysis and thinking on this topic.

The chart below illustrates how open-ended questions seeking information or opinions tend to bring out far more information than do closed-ended questions.

**Closed-ended vs. Open-ended Questions**

| Closed-ended | Possible answers | Open-ended | Possible answers |
|---|---|---|---|
| Do you like Monday morning meetings? | Yes/no | How do you feel about Monday morning meetings? | Well, they do help start the week with a sense of direction, but on the other hand. . . . |
| Did they conduct research first? | Yes/no | What can you tell me about the research behind this finding? | The researchers conducted a six-month study followed by a series of interviews. Here are the results. . . . |
| Did the study have steps? | Yes, three. | What can you tell me about the steps taken in the study? | There were three major steps; the first was . . . the second was. . . . |
| When do you want to have the meeting? | At 8 a.m. on Tuesday. | What are some good times for the meeting? | We could have it early morning on Tuesday or late afternoon on Wednesday. |

■ ■ ■ ■ ■    **EXERCISE**
### Creating Open-Ended Questions

Review the following closed-ended questions and turn them into open-ended questions.

"Do you like working on the team?"

Write an open-ended question: _____

"Did the figures improve in the fourth quarter?"

Write an open-ended question: _____

"Are you ready for the meeting?"

Write an open-ended question: _____

"Has the procurement report been completed?"

Write an open-ended question: _____

"Do you approve of the reorganization plan?"

Write an open-ended question: _____

There are two other important question types. Technically, they are subtypes of open-ended questions, and each has its own distinct form.

### Questions Seeking Opinions

When you need to tap into others' ideas, you ask questions seeking opinions. These are powerful questions to prompt learning, and they also are great alternatives to telling others what to do. Examples include: "What is your perspective on what we talked about in the meeting?" "What did you think about the director's speech?" If you want to encourage an employee to think about meetings and his or her role in them, you could ask opinion questions like:

- ■ "What makes you consider a meeting successful?"
- ■ "What could you have done differently to make the conversation more productive for you?"
- ■ What are your thoughts on the new budget process?

*Questions Addressing Emotions and Nonverbal Communication*

When you want to understand an employee's feelings, ask questions involving emotions and nonverbal communication. These are another subset of open-ended questions. Questions involving emotions and nonverbal communication may come up when an employee:

- Is feeling disappointed in himself or herself
- Lacks self-confidence on a task or project
- Feels nervous in front of a new group
- Is obviously frustrated with the job, team, or project
- Faces work-life imbalance that causes stress.

Is it appropriate to ask employees about how they are feeling emotionally? Yes. Questions about emotions are acceptable and often necessary in the workplace. Tension, stress, and change affect employees' emotions, and strong negative emotions are often underlying causes of poor morale, mistrust, and lack of communication within a team. If you notice symptoms of underperformance in your organization, it may be time to uncover the emotions driving the performance problems. Emotions will naturally surface during coaching conversations as employees talk about what is important to them.

Asking questions relating to expressing emotions, especially empathy, is an important hallmark of resonant, emotionally intelligent leadership, which can "predict effectiveness in professional, management and leadership roles in many sectors."[4] Multiple studies have demonstrated that competencies in emotional and social intelligence are indicators of outstanding performance.[5] One type of empathy is particularly effective—being open and inquiring about how the other person feels.[6]

Clinical psychologist Daniel Shapiro of the Harvard Negotiation Project writes, "You ignore emotions at your peril. Emotions are always present and often affect your experience. You may try to ignore them, but they will not ignore you."[7]

The questions you ask can have a profound effect on employees' motivation and engagement in the workplace during difficult times. For example, when an employee faces a family or health issue, anytime coaches can ask simple open-ended questions such as "How are you coping with your relative's illness?" "Is there anything I can do to help while you are here in the office?" "How can the team best support you during this challenging time?" Asking questions like these shows that you care and are empathetic. Engaging in Anytime Coaching conversations about emotions demonstrates your commitment to enhancing working relationships. Do not shy away from these questions, but approach them with the respect and dignity your employees deserve.

Questions about emotions should not be limited to negative feelings. If an employee is animated or excited, ask about his or her positive emotions. For example: "You seem to really enjoy being on the task force. Why is it so exciting?" Joy, excitement, and passion are positive emotions to address in the practice of inquiring.

As an anytime coach, you will want to build and strengthen these positive emotions in the workplace. Why?

- Positive emotions reinforce and build upon each other.
- Feeling excitement and passion about work increases your employees' commitment to results, the team, and the larger unit.
- Research has shown that one person's positive emotions are contagious.[8] Other employees may "catch" the feeling, leading to even greater collaboration, stronger relationships, and enjoyment of working together.

---

**Boundaries to Asking about Emotions**

Although we recommend having Anytime Coaching conversations about emotions, there are circumstances under which such conversations should not occur. Discussions involving possible organizational liability require an approach different from Anytime Coaching. For example, harassment, discrimination, and other employment biases are topics that employees must first discuss with human resources, legal, or personnel policy specialists because such sensitive and emotional topics could have serious legal liabilities for everyone involved. We understand that you may want to help coach your employees through such emotional situations. But in these cases, it is important to find the right person inside the organization to best help the employee.

Also unsuitable for Anytime Coaching are discussions about mental health issues. If you learn from a coaching conversation that an employee is severely depressed or suffers from another mental health condition, such as anxiety, panic, or bipolar disorder, do not proceed with Anytime Coaching. It is not the role of the anytime coach to serve as the employee's counselor. This is best left to mental health professionals.

Finally, if an employee is uncomfortable talking about emotional or challenging topics or prefers privacy, anytime coaches do not ask questions that might violate the employee's sense of emotional safety and comfort.

Anytime coaches are aware of the referral processes in their organizations, including employee assistance programs or human resource options that can help direct employees to qualified and appropriate assistance.

---

You will recall from Chapter 2 that there is a strong link between emotions and nonverbal communication, but you may notice a lack of congruence or alignment between nonverbal expression and an employee's words. During an Anytime Coaching conversation, if an employee's face shows signs of strong negative emotions (sadness, tension, or anger), but he or she says everything is fine, an open-ended question intended to strengthen the relationship is needed. Some examples:

- "I'm sensing from your facial expression that you are sad. What can you tell me about what happened at the meeting?"

- "I've noticed from the way you're sitting that you may be anxious about the report. If you don't mind sharing, what concerns do you have?"

- "I saw you stop participating at the staff meeting, when you normally are very involved. What caused you to stop participating?"

It is all right for the employee to decline to answer your questions. You will draw upon the complementary practices of observing, listening, and responding to determine what additional questions are needed.

Try to ask questions pertaining to emotions and nonverbal communication at the right time. The following are two situations that call for this kind of questioning:

- If you have noticed a downturn in an employee's job performance, morale, or apparent motivation

- If an employee is obviously angry or avoidant.

### Matching the Purposes and Types of Questions

Now that you understand the three purposes of questions and the four types of questions, you can see that different situations call for different questions. Your job is to choose the best question that will yield the best answer.

- If the purpose of your questions is to get quick information, closed-ended questions are often appropriate.

- If the questions pertain to relationships and solutions, and you want more information or to learn about the employee, open-ended questions are suitable.

- If you want to begin a conversation about an employee's feelings, use open-ended questions.

■ ■ ■ ■ ■ **PRINCIPLE**

Anytime coaches match the purposes and types of question to ensure their questions elicit the best answers.

---

■ ■ ■ ■ ■ **PRACTICE TOOL**
A Challenging Situation

Think of an employee facing a challenging situation at work.

If you engage in an Anytime Coaching conversation with the employee on this particular topic, what potential emotions could emerge (e.g., frustration, anger, sadness)?

_____

_____

_____

How is the situation affecting your employee in the workplace?

_____

_____

_____

Write down three open-ended questions you could ask the employee about the situation.

_____

_____

_____

---

■ ■ **Considering the Receiver of Questions**

The next part of the practice of inquiring focuses on the employee, the receiver of your questions. An employee often responds to questions in predictable patterns, based on how he or she likes to gather information, think, and work. In the practice of inquiring, we seek to ensure that the receiver can understand and respond appropriately to our questions. If you want to challenge or engage the receiver, you may need to ask different or unexpected questions.

As you think through what you would like to ask, try to maintain an attitude of helpfulness and curiosity about the present moment. Be mindful of any tendency toward irritation or annoyance with the employee. Just let such thoughts slide by, replacing them with a focus on what questions would be helpful and what questions would stimulate thought and growth. Keeping a mindful and positive focus on the receiver will help you shape just the right question for the right time.

Take a few moments and think of a question you would like to ask one of your employees about his or her work. Here is a checklist to assist you in analyzing the receiver's needs with regard to questions:

- Am I asking the right person this question? Is it possible that someone else might be a better person to ask?

- What do I already know about this person? How comfortable am I with him or her? Be aware of your relationship with the receiver and the possible impact on the response.

- Is my question likely to make the receiver uncomfortable? Some people are sensitive about certain topics, so it is important to think about this in advance.

- Is he or she quiet? Reluctant to offer information? If so, a closed-ended question will probably yield an inadequate response, so an open-ended question may be necessary.

- Does he or she talk excessively, dominate conversations, or give out too much information? Closed-ended questions, which discourage long replies, may be best.

- Is he or she a detail-oriented person? If so, the receiver is likely to give a detailed or technical answer. Before you ask a question, decide whether you want an in-depth answer or a shorter, closed-ended reply.

- Is he or she a results-oriented person? If so, the receiver is likely to give a short answer focused on outcomes.

■ Is he or she a visionary thinker? He or she will likely give a broader, more creative answer.

■ Does the receiver always expect to have the right answer because he or she has power or a certain position within the organization? Consider power relationships when formulating questions.

■ Does he or she need time to process questions and gather information? Allow the receiver to respond at his or her own pace.

■ Does the receiver get defensive easily? Would this question surprise him or her? If so, it would not be a good idea to ask a question that puts the receiver on the spot in a group setting.

We are not suggesting that you avoid hard or powerful questions, but we urge you to think in advance about how your questions may be received and perceived by the employee.

### ▨ ▨ Choosing the Right Time to Inquire

Having the right targeted, powerful question is important, but timing is equally critical. Have you ever heard someone ask a terrific question at a meeting, but at the wrong time, when no one was paying attention?

Keep these timing considerations in mind:

■ Should I ask the question now, or would it be better to wait?

■ Does the employee's emotional state warrant a cooling-off period?

■ What do I know about my employee's schedule or work habits?

■ Is the employee a morning person, or is the afternoon a better time for an Anytime Coaching conversation?

### Choosing the Right Place to Coach

In general, privacy matters in Anytime Coaching. There may be opportunities to coach in group settings, but the default setting should be a private one. Anytime coaches find the right place to coach.

Here are some questions to think through before a coaching session:

- Can this question be asked in front of a group?
- What kinds of responses might the employee be reluctant to share?
- Are there environmental distractions (noise, distractions, excessive heat or cold)?
- Where is the employee most likely to feel comfortable?

The following example illustrates the importance of timing and location for Anytime Coaching.

Marika, a project manager and new supervisor, now manages two project analysts. Arlene is Marika's manager. While walking down the hall one day, Arlene overhears Marika firing off questions in public to the project analysts. "Did you finish the report? Can I take a look at it?"

Arlene sees Marika grow increasingly impatient as the project analysts both answer "no" to each question. Her interaction with the analysts has revealed little information, so Marika still does not know why the report is incomplete, and she is frustrated.

Arlene recognizes that this is an ideal opportunity for using the practice of inquiring and Anytime Coaching. She asks Marika if she has a few minutes to talk about her conversation with the analysts, and whether Marika minds if Arlene offers some coaching. Marika is eager for assistance and gladly goes into Arlene's office.

Arlene explains the difference between open-ended and closed-ended questions and tells Marika that all the questions she overheard in the hallway were closed-ended. Using open-ended questions, Marika would have gotten more information from the analysts.

Arlene also tells Marika that her questions may have put the analysts on the defensive and made them uncomfortable in public. With encouragement and further questioning from Arlene, Marika comes up with the following list of new open-ended questions:

- How do you feel about the report? Which part do you think is the best and why?
- When will you be comfortable sharing the report with me?
- What concerns do you have at this point that I need to be aware of?
- Can you update me on the timing of when you think you'll have the report completed?

Marika says she is glad to get the Anytime Coaching and will talk to the analysts later—and in private.

---

■ ■ ■ ■ ■   **PRACTICE TOOL**
**Timing and Location of Questions**

Think of a current employee you would like to coach on a specific and targeted issue.

What questions might you ask the employee?

_____

_____

When is the best time to meet with him or her, now or later?

_____

_____

Where is the best place to hold this conversation?

_____

_____

"Confidence, like art, never comes from having all the answers; it comes from being open to all the questions."

—EARL GRAY STEVENS

## Obstacles to Asking Coaching Questions

By now, it should be clear that questions are powerful conversation starters and a bridge to understanding employees and getting information. Yet managers sometimes shrink from asking questions. Why? Usually because they think they do not have time and that asking questions creates risk.

The truth is that you do not have time *not* to ask questions.

### PRINCIPLE

Anytime coaches believe they do not have time *not* to ask good questions and engage in powerful conversations.

Not engaging in Anytime Coaching discourages performance growth and ensures communication is limited and relationships are less productive than they could be. To declare a lack of time is to give up on development and change. Even the busiest of high-performance managers find pockets of time to coach. It does not have to be time-consuming. In fact, productive Anytime Coaching saves management time because through coaching conversations, employees come to truly understand their roles and assignments.

Regarding risk, many people worry about what their colleagues will think of their questions. Do you find it challenging to ask questions at all? Do you avoid certain types of questions and prefer others? You may realize that your own assumptions or fears get in the way of your asking productive questions. Anytime coaches understand that asking the right questions, getting needed information, and achieving better business results are the goal.

An anytime coach who has the clear and calm focus associated with mindfulness will purposely pause before and during a dialogue full of questions. Why? Having a focused presence will decrease the feeling of risk and concern in asking challenging questions. Maintaining calm yet focused attention on the subject at hand and the people in the conversation enables the anytime coach to ask the right questions at the right time.

## Putting It All Together

Here's a checklist of key questions you should ask yourself before engaging in the practice of inquiring:

- What is the purpose of my question? Is it for information, to build a relationship, or to find a solution?
- What type of question do I need to ask (closed-ended, open-ended, seeking opinions, or a question about emotions or nonverbal cues)?
- Who will receive the question?
- What do I need to know about this employee before I ask the question?
- What is the right time to ask the question?
- Where should I ask the question?
- Am I reluctant to ask the question, and if so, why?
- Am I being mindful so I can generate the right questions?

Now that you understand the practice of inquiring, we turn our attention to the practice of listening, through which you will learn to hear and truly understand your employees.

■ ■ ■ ■ ■ ■ ■ ■ ■

"Live your questions now, and perhaps even without knowing it, you will live along some distant day into your answers."

—RAINER MARIA WILKE, 20TH CENTURY GERMAN POET

■ ■ ■ ■ ■ ■ ■ ■ ■

## NOTES

1  Michael Marquardt, *Leading with Questions* (New York: Jossey-Bass, 2005), pp. 171–172.

2  Laura Whitworth, Henry Kimsey-House, and Phil Sandahl, *Co-Active Coaching: New Skills for Coaching People Toward Success in Work and Life* (Palo Alto, CA: Davies-Black Publishing, 1998), p. 238.

3  David Rock, *Quiet Leadership* (New York: HarperCollins, 2006), p. 106.

4  Dr. Richard Boyatzis, "Competencies as a Behavioral Approach to Emotional Intelligence," *Journal of Management and Development*, Vol. 28, No. 9, 2009, p. 749.

5  Ibid.

6  Research of Professor Jean Decety (University of Chicago) and Professor Don Batson (University of Kansas) cited in *the Ivey Business Journal*, February, 2012, p. 2.

7  Roger Fisher and Daniel Shapiro, *Beyond Reason: Using Emotion as You Negotiate* (New York: Penguin Books, 2005), p. 11.

8  Stacey Colino, "That Look—It's Catching! Emotions, Like Germs, Are Easily Transmissible. The Trick is Passing and Receiving the Right Ones," *Washington Post*, May 30, 2006.

## RECOMMENDED READING

Adams, Merrilee. *Change Your Questions, Change Your Life*. San Franscisco, CA: Berrett-Koehler, 2009.

Fisher, Roger, and Daniel Shapiro. *Beyond Reason: Using Emotions as You Negotiate*. New York: Penguin Books, 2005.

Hatfield, Elaine, John T. Cacioppo, and Richard L. Rapson. *Emotional Contagion: Studies in Emotional and Social Interaction*. New York: Press Syndicate of the University of Cambridge, 1994.

Marquardt, Michael. *Leading with Questions*. San Francisco: Jossey-Bass, 2005.

Whitney, Diana, David Cooperrider, Amanda Trosten-Bloom, and Brian S. Kaplin, *Encyclopedia of Positive Questions*. Euclid, OH: Lakeshore Communications, 2002.

Whitworth, Laura, Henry Kimsey-House, and Phil Sandahl. *Co-Active Coaching: New Skills for Coaching People Toward Success in Work and Life*. Palo Alto, CA: Davies-Black Publishing, 1998.

# 4 The Practice of Listening

> "No one ever listened themselves out of a job."
>
> —CALVIN COOLIDGE, 13TH PRESIDENT OF THE UNITED STATES

Anytime coaches build on skillful observing and inquiring by enhancing their listening skills. Ordinary listening is not enough; anytime coaches employ *extreme* listening.

## Extreme Listening

What is extreme listening? It is the ability to listen without bias, with the voice in your head turned off, and with complete attention on what the speaker is saying and what he or she means. Extreme listening is particularly difficult in today's work environment because of the omnipresence of technology, the fast pace, and constant interruptions. The myth of multitasking has encouraged people to pretend to listen to others while texting, reading email, or doing a variety of other tasks. But with extreme listening, you can *only* listen—with complete and total attention on the person speaking to you.

Think about it: Without extreme listening, how can we ask our employees the most appropriate questions? What we observe with our eyes is only part of the picture. We might unwittingly misinterpret an employee's words if we do not listen fully. Extreme listening is the prerequisite for any effective conversation. And in today's world, conversations are the means by which much work is accomplished. Improving our work conversations rests squarely on being able to listen intensely with the intention to understand.

Extreme listening is also effective in taming the FRG and helping you stay focused when the brain's default network kicks in or experiences cognitive capacity overload. By cultivating presence, awareness, and focus, managers begin to practice extreme listening—and get results.

To truly listen to others, we need to be focused on them and what they are saying—and on nothing else. In this age of multitasking, how is this possible? One approach to increasing our listening capacity is to enhance our overall ability to focus and hold attention. A regular mindfulness practice will help build this capacity for deliberate attention.

Central to a mindfulness practice is holding your focus on something as simple as your breathing—and away from stress-inducing thoughts. Studies of brief mindfulness meditation training have shown reduced psychological stress reactivity.[1] Brain images of subjects trained in mindfulness show that "mindfulness practice improved the focusing of attentional resources."[2]

To get an idea of how this works, just think about doing repeated bicep curls during a physical workout, and then think of repeated efforts to focus your attention on your breathing as the "reps" for strengthening the attention "muscle." With continued practice, your ability to hold attention without distracting thoughts will increase, as will your listening skill. With a habit of mindfulness, your ability to hold focused attention and your listening ability will both expand.

---

**On Multitasking**

Anytime Coaches know they should not send a text, check their phone, or engage in any form of multitasking during extreme listening. Why? Because multitasking is a myth. The brain cannot perform two or more tasks simultaneously but instead will rapidly switch back and forth between tasks. Switching between tasks may occur quickly (a few tenths of a second), but will make it harder to block distractions and will ultimately slow down efficiency.[3]

According to researchers, multitasking can reduce productivity by as much as 40 percent. "In 2010, a study by neuroscientists at the French medical research agency showed that when people focus on two tasks simultaneously, each side of the brain tackles a different task. This suggests a two-task limit on what the human brain can handle. Taking on more tasks increases the likelihood of errors."[4] Focusing fully on the speaker requires your full attention without distractions, as do all the practices of Anytime Coaching.

---

■ ■ ■ ■ ■ ■  **PRINCIPLE**

Extreme listening is listening with complete attention to what the speaker is saying and intends.

## ■ ■ ■  The Practice of Listening

Listening is closely linked to the practice of observing. Watching what others do and being sensitive to nonverbal cues are important skills for anytime coaches; think of listening as a "sister skill" to observing. Listening focuses specifically on the words people say and on the themes and patterns of the stories they tell.

Listening and the practice of inquiring also go hand in hand. When we ask questions of others, the implication is, of course, that we are interested in their answers. So we have an *obligation* to listen—truly listen. Listening gives you hooks on which to hang your next question, a paraphrase, or a request for clarification. Without extreme listening, we often carry on conversations in response to what is in our own heads; we miss out on the vital information gained by truly hearing others' words. If you do not listen fully to what is being said, it's all too easy to respond in a way that makes little sense or is even offensive to the other person. Anytime coaches know that this is neither a good use of time nor a good way to build strong working relationships.

The practice of listening is also enhanced by mindful observation. As Rebecca Shafir writes in *The Zen of Listening*:

> As it pertains to listening [mindfulness] meditation allows our minds to hear with less distortion new ideas and points of view. After a few weeks of practice you will notice that you are less anxious when hearing ideas that differ from your point of view. Your ability to concentrate is deeper and more enduring, and with anxiety under control, you can better focus your attention on getting and retaining the message. Moreover, regular meditation practice improves your attitude, the ability to deploy attention, and sets the stage for mindful listening.[5]

On the path to becoming an anytime coach, you will need to learn how to:

1. *Prepare for extreme listening.* We will explore your listening biases and different ways of viewing workplace conversations, and we will help you check your assumptions and quiet the voice in your head.

2. *Focus on the person speaking.* You will learn how to consider your reactions and step into a neutral listening zone.

3. *Listen for "stories."* We will help you recognize and deal effectively with the stories employees tell, urging you to listen for "good stories."

Anytime coaches realize that extreme listening makes the person you are listening to feel good. Take a moment and think about a supervisor or manager, or even a friend or relative, who took the time to listen fully to your ideas. Do you remember how good it felt to be heard and understood? Would you like to create the same good feeling of being acknowledged and appreciated in the people around you?

Dr. James Pennebaker found that when people were given a chance to discuss a stressful event in their lives with willing listeners, their blood pressure decreased. He also reported that having a confidant strengthened the immune system. Being heard lifts self-esteem; we feel important when someone takes the time to hear us out.[6]

The practice of listening takes work and time. As a senior vice president at a Fortune 500 company explained: " Listening was one of the practices I had to work on the most to become an anytime coach. As the boss you assume you always have to have the answer. I realized that this is not my value to my employees. I need to listen more and ask questions—that is my role and greatest value as an executive."

Imagine the positive impact on your workplace and day-to-day performance if employees had a constant sense of being heard and understood. Anytime Coaching practices will help you make this happen.

"Listening is such a simple act. It requires us to be present, and that takes practice, but we don't have to do anything else. We don't have to advise, or coach, or sound wise. We just have to be willing to sit there and listen."

—MARGARET J. WHEATLEY, AUTHOR AND
ORGANIZATIONAL BEHAVIOR CONSULTANT

## Preparing for Extreme Listening

We will examine a number of ways to help you prepare for extreme listening. You will learn about:

- Uncovering and managing your listening biases
- Examining and changing how you view your work conversations
- Checking your assumptions
- Doing a "head check" before beginning Anytime Coaching conversations.

Let's begin by learning to uncover your listening biases.

"Few people . . . have had much training in listening. Living in a competitive culture, most of us are most of the time chiefly concerned with getting our own views across, and we tend to find other people's speeches a tedious interruption of our own ideas."

—S. I. HAYAKAWA, 20TH CENTURY AMERICAN PSYCHOLOGIST,
TEACHER, WRITER, AND U.S. SENATOR

## Uncovering and Managing Your Listening Biases

Most of us have biases in our listening styles. We tend to listen *for* something, or for a specific reason. Have you ever known people who seem to rebut or contradict most of what you say? Their listening bias is that they are listening for an inconsistency, an error, or a chance to correct you. Have you ever known someone who seemed to listen only long enough to find something funny in what was said? People with this listening bias are listening for a chance to make a wisecrack or to amuse the crowd. And you probably know people who listen so carefully that they analyze your word choices or the structure of every sentence. Such people are listening for meaning, accuracy, and logical correctness.

Common listening biases include:

- Listening to find exceptions, argument points, or contradictions
- Listening to find something amusing or entertaining
- Listening for accuracy or correctness
- Listening for the big picture or themes
- Listening for a "problem" (whether one exists or not!)
- Listening for facts, learning, or retention (especially during a lecture or presentation that is critical for work or study)
- Listening for mood, nuance, or the unspoken story
- Listening for a place to interject your own thoughts
- Listening to hear information that confirms what you think or believe.

Such listening biases are quite normal; you can probably identify your own from this list.[7]

One of the most common listening biases is listening to validate what you already think is true. Psychologists call this "confirmation bias," the tendency to look for and find support for a point of view you have already adopted. A tool that helps explain confirmation bias is known as "the ladder of inference." As the brain moves up the ladder from raw information to labels, assumptions, and broader beliefs, the brain is conditioned to make certain choices. The brain will automatically select something that confirms assumptions and beliefs it already has.

Describing the ladder of inference in *The Fifth Discipline Fieldbook*, Richard Ross writes, "Our beliefs influence what data we select next time."[8] Confirmation bias can create deeply embedded brain pathways that reinforce established listening patterns and preferences, which explains why extreme listening is tough work that requires practice.

We select what we pay attention to, add our own meanings, make assumptions, draw conclusions, and form beliefs; our listening is often clouded by all these mental processes.[9] The implication for Anytime Coaching is that we need to be mindful of the opinions and judgments we have already formed about our employees and their work because those opinions and judgments will steer our listening and observation directly to data (their words and actions) that support our pre-existing opinions and judgments.

Cultivating the ability to observe one's own state of mind is a key skill to help overcome listening biases. It will increase the ability to realize when we are simply trying to confirm our own biases by seeking only data that supports pre-existing beliefs. Increased awareness means we can deliberately listen for other points of view without the jarring feeling that accompanies having our own beliefs shaken.

One of the most important things anytime coaches can do is monitor their listening biases. With extreme listening, you will no longer:

■ Listen just for evidence to prove your point

■ Listen to prove the other person is wrong

■ Listen just to appear to be listening

■ Listen to hear information that confirms what you think or believe.

Jeff Jones, Managing Director at Bank of the West, describes a time when he realized the importance of becoming an extreme listener:

> *One of my biggest "aha" leadership moments took place working with one of my employees. He was not a great talker and I found him very hard to listen to. He spoke extremely slowly and had a thick accent. At some point, I realized I needed to be quiet and just listen. For this employee, I had to put away my computer and physically sit next to him to really concentrate on his speaking. As it turns out, this employee was brilliant and one of the smartest technical workers I have ever had on my team. He had a thousand solutions that I would have never availed myself of if I had not slowed down and listened to him at his own pace. I had so many listening biases to overcome about this amazing employee.*

Jeff further explains what happens to so many senior leaders and managers: "Listening is hard for me to do. I have to fight the urge to talk and instead become an extreme listener. I am a storyteller, and I have had to train myself to become a listener. It was worth it."

■ ■ ■ ■ ■ ■ **PRINCIPLE**

Anytime coaches are aware of and manage their listening biases to achieve extreme listening.

Shifting your routine listening to the extreme listening style of an anytime coach will require time, practice, and *change*.

### Examining and Changing How You View Your Work Conversations

Step back and consider how you view your work conversations. Do you see them as an opportunity to help your employees? As a way to learn more? As daily challenges to your expertise and competence? As subtle traps during which you might say the wrong thing? As a chance to show how much you know? Even if you don't view your work conversations in any of these ways, you must examine your perspective on the conversations with the employees you will coach. Why? Because how you view the conversations will greatly influence your listening patterns.

Think about not having any opinion at all about an upcoming conversation; instead, consider it a data-gathering exercise, as if you were an anthropologist or an investigative reporter. Ask yourself, "What is happening here?" "What new data are being presented" "Did I just hear a strongly held opinion, or was there a factual basis for what was said?" "Was that a sweeping conclusion being drawn from a single data point?" Such questions arise from a mind that is not focused on being right or is in search of winning arguments, but is instead focused on viewing every conversation as simply new data to be considered in the moment. We call this "nonjudgmental curiosity."

"Be curious, not judgmental."

—WALT WHITMAN, 19TH CENTURY AMERICAN POET

■ ■ ■ ■ ■ ■   **PRACTICE TOOL**
Evaluating Work Conversations

Think about a recent conversation you had with an employee that did not go well and that you may have to repeat with him or her. Use the Conversation Tracker tool to evaluate your conversation and gather your thoughts for your next talk with the employee.

| Conversation Tracker | | |
|---|---|---|
| Conversation: | Other party: | Date: |
| Purpose of conversation | ☐ Information gathering<br>☐ Clarification | ☐ Problem/solution<br>☐ New assignment |
| | | ☐ Other _____ |
| My thoughts before the conversation: | | |
| What I hoped to achieve: | | |
| What happened during the conversation: | | |
| What I said… | What he or she said… | The real message was… |
| | | |
| How effective was the conversation?<br>1=Very ineffective, 2 = Somewhat ineffective, 3 = Moderately effective, 4 = Somewhat effective, 5=Extremely effective | | |
| My thoughts after the conversation: | | |
| What I might do differently next time: | | |
| What possible listening biases should I be aware of? | | |

*Nonjudgmental Curiosity*

One way to change how we view our work conversations is to cultivate a sense of nonjudgmental curiosity: listening with no preconceived notions. This means turning off the voice in your head before a conversation even begins. Use the mindfulness exercise "Taking Two Quiet Minutes" at the end of Chapter 2 to calm any lingering tension you might have about an upcoming conversation. Being more present, aware, and focused will increase your ability to exercise nonjudgmental curiosity.

So instead of thinking, "She never tries anything new," you might think, "I wonder how she will approach this?" Instead of thinking, "This employee is so combative," you might think, "I wonder what he will think of this idea?"

If your workplace is very fast-paced, you might think that you just do not have the extra time it takes to listen deeply. While pressure to produce may be a constant in your workplace, this kind of listening prevents the inevitable misunderstandings that come from *not* listening deeply—and thus saves time in the end. When an anytime coach listens in this way, his or her employees will sense more openness and genuine interest. An employee who is listened to in this way is more likely to be fully engaged in the conversation.

■ ■ ■ ■ ■ ■ **PRINCIPLE**

Extreme listeners exhibit nonjudgmental curiosity during work conversations.

*Another View of Work Conversations: Are You a Teller or an Asker?*

Managers who are "tellers" tend to think of work conversations as opportunities to share what they know, give advice, and advocate for their points of view. They listen long enough to get sufficient information from the speaker, and then give advice or directions. People who report to tellers learn to stand by for the next set of opinions or orders. They soon learn that their ideas and expertise are secondary to those of the teller. Too much telling conveys a lack of interest in what others have to say. Such obvious lack of interest in others' ideas leads to employees' eventual disengagement and lowered productivity. When the tendency to tell takes over, extreme listening takes a back seat.

"Askers," on the other hand, view work conversations as opportunities to learn from others. They demonstrate curiosity about others' ideas and experiences. They take the time to form thoughtful questions and, just as importantly, they give time for the speaker to think and respond. While askers may seem like ideal conversation partners, they also must take special care to exhibit extreme listening. The very act of asking a question implies that you are interested in the speaker's response. On the other hand, bombarding people with questions without taking the time to listen communicates a lack of interest in what they have to say.

Reflect on your workplace conversations with your employees. Are you a teller, always ready with a solution or the right answer just in time? Or do you ask thought-provoking questions, eager to learn something new? The wisdom is in knowing when to be a teller and when to be an asker. Anytime coaches learn to balance necessary telling with insightful questioning. In all conversations, anytime coaches demonstrate extreme listening before telling or asking.

Imagine a continuum with tellers on one side and askers on the other.

| Tellers | People who balance telling and asking behaviors | Askers |
| --- | --- | --- |

| What tellers do | What people who balance behaviors do | What askers do |
| --- | --- | --- |
| • Listen long enough to form advice or direction<br>• Assume that advice and direction are what the speaker wants or needs<br>• Want to be seen as knowledgeable and wise | • Shift between telling and asking<br>• Know when advice and direction are appropriate<br>• Know when asking questions is appropriate<br>• Ask speakers if they want advice<br>• Make clear when they are giving direction. For example: "Here is what I want you to do." "These are the steps I want you to follow."<br>• After giving advice or direction, ask open-ended feedback questions: "What do you think?" "How does that sound?" | • Listen with open curiosity and a spirit of learning<br>• Form thoughtful questions based on what the speaker has said<br>• Want to know more before sharing viewpoints or directions |

| Risks of being a teller | | Risks of being an asker |
| --- | --- | --- |
| • Can give the appearance of not listening, because their responses often do not acknowledge what the speaker has said<br>• Convey a lack of interest in the other person's point of view and knowledge | | • Can overwhelm with too many questions<br>• Can be so intent on the next question that they do not truly hear the answer to the prior question |

| Recommendations for change | | Recommendations for change |
| --- | --- | --- |
| • Must exercise extreme listening to hear more than the opportunities to give advice or direction<br>• Must develop curiosity about others' ideas and experiences | | • Must pause to hear every answer without bias or preconceived opinions<br>• Must acknowledge answers and affirm them with paraphrases or summarizing statements that demonstrate extreme listening |

■ ■ ■ ■ ■ ■ **PRINCIPLE**

Anytime coaches balance telling and asking behaviors while exhibiting extreme listening.

## Checking Your Assumptions

Assumptions are beliefs that underlie our actions. They also determine how we listen. If we assume we have all the answers, we may act as tellers at work. If we assume our workers lack necessary skills or knowledge, we may help them too much or give them too few challenges. If we assume our employees are creative and motivated, we become curious and inquisitive managers, asking about their ideas—and exhibiting extreme listening. If we assume that gathering many ideas leads to the best solutions, we treat each worker as the owner of part of the answer and respectfully encourage him or her to share ideas—while practicing extreme listening.

A couple of key assumptions underlie all pieces of the Anytime Coaching model—especially the practice of listening:

- *The best work often results from a collaborative process.* While there may be an organizational hierarchy, and some people do have more expertise than others, drawing upon everyone's best thinking yields better and more sustainable performance.
- *People grow by doing.* When people try new things, experiment, and create new outcomes, they expand their overall capacity to think, perform, and achieve results.

Listening with these assumptions will dramatically transform how you hear others. Even if colleagues around you do not seem to share these underlying beliefs, you can still model extreme listening behaviors. Through your example, you will open their eyes and ears to the benefits of extreme listening.

## ■ ■ ■ ■ ■ ■ **PRINCIPLE**

Anytime coaches believe the best work often results from a collaborative process and listen with this in mind.

### ■ ■ Doing a Head Check

The "voice in your head" is the mental noise that gets in the way of nonjudgmental curiosity. Even if you are fully aware of your assumptions and have adopted a positive view of workplace conversations, you can still have a voice in your head saying unhelpful things: "I don't have time for this conversation—I have a deadline in two hours." "If I talk to this employee, his negativity will drag me down." "I am not sure I have the skills needed for this project." Remember that the voice in your head is likely the voice of the FRG, which always wants you to move as quickly as possible and discourages you from doing a head check because it takes precious time.

---

How Mindfulness Helps in Doing a Head Check

When you have established a habit of mindful meditation, your brain can engage the "muscle" of attention by directing the mind's attention to a chosen focal point, allowing unhelpful and distracting thoughts to simply drift away. Routine practice will make you more agile at harnessing your attention and directing it purposefully toward something else, like another person talking. A brain that has habitually practiced mindful meditation will find it easier to focus solely on the present moment and allow unhelpful thoughts about the past or future to pass by without disrupting the practice of extreme listening.

---

Be aware that the voice in your head can be tamed—but only *you* can do it. Consciously choose to see workplace conversations as vibrant, energizing, and as opportunities for learning and growth. Instead of "I wish I weren't talking to this person," you can intentionally think, "I wonder what contribution this person can make to the project design?" Instead of "I am not sure I can be an anytime coach," you can deliberately think, "I am learning to be an anytime coach." When you quiet the voice in your head and replace distracting messages with ones that support Anytime Coaching, you will find that extreme listening is the natural result.

■ ■ ■ ■ ■ ■ **PRINCIPLE**

Anytime coaches listen for opportunities to give people a chance to grow.

■ ■ ■ ■ ■ ■ ■ ■ ■

"We will be more successful in all our endeavors if we can let go of the habit of running all the time, and take little pauses to relax and re-center ourselves...."

—THICH NHAT HANH, 21ST CENTURY PHILOSOPHER

■ ■ ■ ■ ■ **PRACTICE TOOL**
## Doing a Head Check

Before you even begin a coaching conversation, practice doing your own head check:

☐ What listening biases do I have?

_____

_____

☐ What am I already assuming about this situation or this employee?

_____

_____

☐ What is the voice in my head telling me?

_____

_____

☐ What mental noise must I ignore to listen fully to what my employee says?

_____

_____

☐ How am I feeling emotionally? Upset? Energized? Anxious? Something else?

_____

_____

☐ Am I ready to learn something?

_____

_____

☐ Am I ready to work *with* another person?

_____

_____

☐ Am I listening with nonjudgmental curiosity?

_____

_____

Once you become aware of your unhelpful assumptions and listening habits, you become more able to let them go. You become accustomed to using extreme listening, and your ability to hear what others are saying increases exponentially. Extreme listening can be especially challenging in work environments in which there is a great deal of activity and many people interacting at once. But it is in these very busy workplaces that extreme listening does the most good. It adds a measure of sanity and a sense of mutual respect to the workplace. Remember to engage PAF—be *present*, *aware*, and *focused*—during extreme listening.

In a workplace full of extreme listeners, fewer misunderstandings arise, and staff make fewer poor decisions based on biased and un-skilled listening. As a result, you will start to notice day-to-day performance improvement.

■ ■ ■ ■ ■  **PRACTICE TOOL**
Preparing to Listen

Think about an important, substantive conversation you will soon have with an employee. Ask yourself:

What are your assumptions about the employee?

_____

_____

What are your assumptions about the situation or problem?

_____

_____

What listening bias might you have to overcome?

_____

_____

What is the voice in your head saying about the upcoming conversation?

_____

_____

How might this conversation go if you enter it with nonjudgmental curiosity?

_____

_____

What do you hope will happen during the conversation?

_____

_____

How can you think differently about the conversation so that you can practice extreme listening?

_____

_____

As you have prepared for extreme listening, you have dropped your listening biases, examined how you view work conversations, uncovered your assumptions, and done a head check. What's next?

## Focusing on the Person Speaking

You are ready to listen and learn, and the voice in your head is turned off. Now focus only on the person to whom you are speaking. Practice the observation skills from Chapter 2. For example, one way to calm yourself when talking to someone who is agitated is the breathing exercise in Chapter 2, "Taking Two Quiet Minutes." You will be better equipped to stay less reactive when surprised by someone else's sudden anxiety.

Be ready to hear the person's words while paying special attention to emotional and nonverbal cues, including facial expressions, movements, posture, and voice. Notice whether he or she seems relaxed, confused, anxious, or angry. Remember that a speaker's words convey only a small portion of the overall message.

### Considering Your Reactions

Next, be aware of your own reaction to the other person's emotional state. For example, if talking with an agitated person upsets you, acknowledge this and do what you can to calm yourself, or delay the conversation until you both are ready. Why? You will have a stronger chance of a positive outcome if at least one person is calm. What if your employee seems too relaxed, while you feel that more energy should be devoted to an issue? Your judgment of her ("She's too laid-back!") may keep you from fully hearing her. Be aware of your judgment and then mentally step into a neutral space where you say to yourself, "OK, that's just my opinion. Now I have to focus on what we are going to do about this issue."

Research on emotional intelligence tells us that the twin abilities of self-awareness and self-management are keys to success at work.[10] They are also essential for all practices in the Anytime Coaching model, but particularly for listening. As an extreme listener, you must be aware of your own emotional tendencies and then manage those tendencies so they do not interfere with your goals. Then you must become aware of other people's states of mind and emotions so you can interact purposefully and respond to them appropriately. In the practice of listening, every conversation is a new opportunity to be self-aware, to self-manage, to be aware of others, and to create positive relationships.

Moving through this four-part process (illustrated below) is a constant challenge for even the most emotionally intelligent people. Self-awareness and awareness of others' emotions will help you notice that there is so much more to most conversations than just the words. Self-management and relationship-building skills mitigate the effect of others' emotional states on you, so that you do not become reactive and lose your own emotional footing.

When you put it all together, you will become an extreme listener by being aware of your own and others' emotional positions during any conversation *and* consciously managing your reactions to build better relationships.

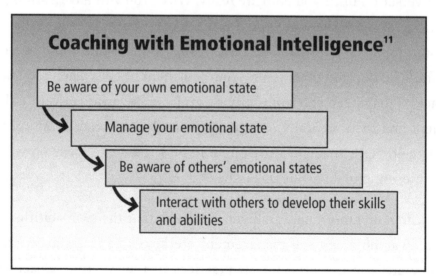

**Coaching with Emotional Intelligence**[11]

Be aware of your own emotional state

Manage your emotional state

Be aware of others' emotional states

Interact with others to develop their skills and abilities

## Stepping into a Neutral Zone

Anytime Coaching enables you to observe your own emotions and manage your reactions while being aware of others' emotions. You do this by stepping into a neutral zone where you are completely open to the specifics of what your conversation partner is saying. In this neutral zone, you will be listening with nonjudgmental curiosity. Neutral-zone listening is like tuning in clearly to a radio station; you will hear no interference from other frequencies. Studies suggest that your ability to reach the nonreactive neutral zone is enhanced by a regular practice of mindfulness.[12]

Here are some tips to help you stay in this neutral zone:

- Set aside any mental judgments you have made about the person or the situation.
- Commit to hearing all of what the other person says.
- Focus on getting more facts and asking clarification questions.
- Work to move the conversation forward.
- Be aware of your own and others' emotions.

There may be additional benefits to strengthening your mindful presence and stepping into a neutral zone. Researchers from the University of Wisconsin used powerful brain scanners to examine expert practitioners of focused meditation and found "demonstrable changes in the networks of the brain that are known to modulate attention."[13]

Jacque Hightower, a senior leader in a public sector organization, described how stepping into the neutral zone and focusing on the person speaking works for him:

*Recently, I knew we were going to miss a deadline on an important system implementation, and I felt strongly we had to push the date back. I knew it could be a challenging conversation with my boss.*

*Rather than anticipating what she might say, or feeling the emotions that were likely, I just went to a neutral space. I said, "Here are the facts, here are the challenges, the risks, and mitigation strategies." She had questions, and when I was able to answer those questions without getting into my own emotions, she agreed to push the deadline back a week.*

*In this deadline-driven environment, we often act like we are listening when we are texting, emailing, or reading emails when we are talking to staff, giving them the impression that we don't care, that we are not interested in their ideas. Now when people come into my office, I lock my screen, turn my chair all the way around, move my papers, look them in the eye, and just listen to them. I make sure I am aware of my body language, my reactions, and my nonverbals and I make sure I keep all that in check while I listen. One of my staff told me that one of her colleagues said, "The thing with Jacque is that he actually listens and he acts like he cares about what we're saying. . . he's really hearing us."*

### Staying in the Neutral Zone When Emotions Run Strong

Emotions are ever-present in Anytime Coaching conversations. The work of Albert Mehrabian[14] shows that physical and vocal cues may be more influential than words during a conversation. When practicing extreme listening, if you notice that you (or your conversation partner) have a strong emotional reaction, what do you do to stay in the neutral zone?

Try labeling what you are feeling. Relabeling emotions is not only useful during Anytime Coaching conversations, it also helps quiet the more primitive portion of your brain that reacts while you are listening, keeping you away from the neutral zone. This will also help the other person understand your response better.

Neuroscientist Dr. Matthew Lieberman of UCLA has shown that re-labeling emotions to help stay in the neutral zone creates "implicit self-control." In brain scanner studies, Lieberman found that relabeling and reappraisal reduce activity in the primitive portion of our brain, a section of the limbic system known as the amygdala, and activate a portion of the prefrontal cortex (specifically the right ventral lateral area).[15]

Another approach in the midst of a difficult, "must-have-it-now" conversation is to encourage open communication by making simple, factual—and nonjudgmental—"I" statements such as "I am confused right now." Or "I'm troubled by what's happening here."

If you or your employee are overcome with emotion—and you know you have left the neutral zone—it may be difficult, if not impossible, to practice extreme listening and have a productive Anytime Coaching conversation. Deal with the emotions first, and then agree to address the work issue in a calmer moment.

### ▪ ▪ ▪ ▪ ▪ ▪ PRINCIPLE

Anytime coaches listen for emotion—others' and their own—and step into a neutral zone, ready to hear what the other person is saying.

## ▪ ▪ ▪ Listening for the Story

As you get better at extreme listening, you may begin to notice patterns. You might realize that certain employees have a "theme"— a "story" they tell again and again. Why is this true? All of us see ourselves a certain way, and we make certain judgments about the world we inhabit. Our view of ourselves and those judgments are determined by a wide variety of factors, including our upbringing, what we have been taught by others, our early jobs, and other experiences.

How we see ourselves and the world around us heavily influences how we present ourselves to others and the stories we tell over and over again.

Rather than delve into the reasons people develop their world views and the resulting stories they tell, we will focus on developing the listening skills that recognize such stories. We will learn how to work with employees who seem to present the same story repeatedly. We will identify some common stories you may hear at work and suggest ways to coach through these stories.

Coaching empowers employees to take responsibility for the work that must be done and to take new actions to complete that work. Anytime Coaching also helps the employee feel valued and respected, ultimately leading to day-to-day performance improvement. These coaching conversations can occur any and every day, and may need to be repeated several times before someone with a common story begins to see—and *do*—things differently.

Some common stories heard in the workplace are:

- "Poor me!"
- "They did it."
- "No big deal."
- "I have the answer."
- "The sky is falling!"
- "I will fix it."

| "Poor Me" | When Hearing This Story, an Anytime Coach: |
|---|---|
| **Unspoken Theme:** Gloom and doom, powerlessness. Work and life are difficult and oppressive.<br><br>**What the Employee Says:** I can't get a response, the rules changed, it's headaches all around. This always happens to me. The deck is stacked against me. | • Uses questions to isolate the facts about specific situations<br>• Remains empathetic without buying into the story<br>• Asks about ways to see things differently<br>• Involves the individual in creating short-term solutions for everyday, ordinary issues<br>• Asks for a commitment to follow up on good ideas for solving immediate problems and eliminating roadblocks |
| **"They Did It"** | **When Hearing This Story, an Anytime Coach:** |
| **Unspoken Theme:** Lack of accountability and control. Blame is external.<br><br>**What the Employee Says:** I couldn't complete the task because my coworker (or the traffic, or the software, etc.)…. I can't help it if someone else…. They're out to get me. | • Asks open-ended questions to understand the full picture, rather than buy into the blame game<br>• Listens with care<br>• Probes for the employee's ideas about eliminating issues before they arise<br>• Acknowledges that sometimes unforeseen circumstance do occur and must be handled<br>• Encourages the employee to commit to taking responsibility, moving forward, and owning his or her part in the problem and solution |
| **"No Big Deal"** | **When Hearing This Story, an Anytime Coach:** |
| **Unspoken Theme:** Denial of real issues, coupled with lack of results. Dodges responsibility.<br><br>**What the Employee Says:** If you (or she, or everyone else) would just follow my advice, this would be solvable. I don't know what you're talking about. This is a minor glitch, easily solved. I don't see what the problem is here. I don't have any problems. | • Asks deeper questions to understand why the employee believes there is no real problem and listens respectfully<br>• Presents available data confirming that a serious situation exists and needs to be addressed<br>• Avoids contradicting and lets the data speak for itself<br>• When necessary, points out the true proportions of the dilemma and the likely consequences of not solving it well<br>• Inquires about new ways to handle the situation in light of the data<br>• When appropriate, invites others into the solution-making conversation |

| "I Have the Answer" | When Hearing This Story, an Anytime Coach: |
|---|---|
| **Unspoken Theme:** Knows it all, has done it all, needs no input.<br><br>**What the Employee Says:** Clearly, we just need to.... I've been around here a long time and know what works and what doesn't work. This is the one right way to do this. Here's the answer—end of story. | • Offers appreciation for the employee's high level of experience and confidence<br>• Listens attentively and respectfully to the recommended solution<br>• Probes for why the employee believes this is the best solution<br>• Urges the employee to invite other colleagues affected by the situation to share their points of view<br>• When appropriate, directs the employee to involve additional people in crafting a "fix" |
| "The Sky Is Falling" | When Hearing This Story, an Anytime Coach: |
| **Unspoken Theme:** Panic in the face of ordinary obstacles. The smallest bumps in the road are major roadblocks. Daily events seem like emergencies. Everything is a tragedy in the making.<br><br>**What the Employee Says:** We'll never make the deadline with this. . . . There's no way to get this done. . . . We're only getting further behind. Can you believe what just happened? | • Does not react to the employee's panic mode; stays calm; is empathetic without buying into the hysteria<br>• Focuses on uncovering the facts of the situation<br>• Asks questions that put the situation in perspective and help the employee see that things are not so dire<br>• Collaborates in developing solutions to reassure the employee that he or she is not alone in this<br>• Commits to following up and then reinforces calm and competent approaches to handling difficulties |
| "I Will Fix It" | When Hearing This Story, an Anytime Coach: |
| **Theme:** Takes control of solving an issue, whether equipped or informed enough to do so. Keeps others from getting involved. Stays in charge when teamwork or collaboration is needed. Takes credit for "fixing it."<br><br>**What the Employee Says:** I'll take care of it right away. Trust me, I will handle this. Just let me do this. | • Engages in sharing ideas for resolving the issue to assess the employee's ability to do so<br>• Probes for whether others might also have valid perspectives on the situation<br>• Encourages the employee to step back and look at the issue from the standpoint of others<br>• When appropriate, directs the employee to have conversations with others to work out a solution based on multiple sources of input<br>• Follows up to assess the success of "the fix"; solicits and gives feedback on what went well and what could have been done differently |

## ▪▪▪ Talking about the Story Itself

If an employee tells you the same story repeatedly, consider intervening—talking about the story itself. Let's suppose Justin relies on the "they did it" story. You might say, "Justin, I would like to share with you something I have noticed lately. Yesterday, you said your work would be late because a coworker failed to get you the information you needed. On Tuesday, you said your report was incomplete because the computer crashed. And today, you could not respond to my inquiry for the latest monthly update because you said accounting was behind. I see a common thread here. Do you?"

Listen to what the person says in response. Stop. Listen some more. Then describe what you notice: "What I hear is a similar story each time. Do you see what I mean?" The conversation will mean more to the employee if your questions lead to him or her seeing and labeling the story. If this does not work, then describe what you are hearing: "I am hearing that you do not get your work done on time because of someone or something else. Is that right?" Even if the employee replies, "Yes, that's right," continue with the Anytime Coaching practice of inquiring, particularly asking open-ended questions.

You may ask questions like these when you think you are hearing a common workplace story:

- ▪ What might you do differently to get a better outcome?
- ▪ What are you going to do next time so the same thing does not happen again?
- ▪ What would be different if you accepted help?
- ▪ What can you control here?
- ▪ What's possible in the time remaining?
- ▪ What would happen if you changed your point of view?

■ What if you believed that there will be no negative conse-
quences?

■ What if you asked other people questions about what's important to them?

■ How will you know if you have fixed the situation?

■ How will you approach a similar situation next time?

■ How are you handling that now?

■ How might others view your proposal?

■ ■ ■ ■ ■ ■ **PRINCIPLE**

Through extreme listening, anytime coaches recognize
common employee "stories" and guide employees to new
ways of thinking, speaking, and acting.

## ■ ■ ■ Listening for Good Stories Too

Anytime coaches can help employees who tell unproductive stories
develop new perspectives, and perhaps even new stories. You will
also hear some "good" stories from your colleagues and employees—
stories that make work flow well and working relationships thrive.
These do not require any intervention at all, and it is important to
acknowledge and reinforce them. Here are a few kinds of stories that
benefit the workplace:

■ *"I do what I say."* Those who tell this story are deliberate
about what they say and what they commit to, and they reli-
ably follow through on their pledges. If you consistently hear
this story, acknowledge it and voice appreciation. "I really like
the way you followed through on this difficult commitment,
Raj."

- *"I treat people with respect."* These employees listen carefully and consider seriously the ideas and proposals of others. They refrain from snap judgments, gossip, and accusations. Let these people know you appreciate their respectful approach. "Yvette, I have noticed that you do not get drawn into office gossip and instead keep your attention on what needs to be done. Your positive example is helpful."

- *"I welcome others' ideas."* Employees who tell this story do not have all the answers, but they actively try to learn about others' ideas and experiences. They are not defensive when others examine their proposals and ideas. If you consistently hear this story, make a point of reinforcing it. You might tell your employee, "I noticed that you paid very close attention to everyone's ideas in today's meeting, Emilio. And you were open to others' critique of your proposal. This really helps everyone feel respected, and I appreciate it."

These are just a few examples of positive stories we may hear when we listen closely to our colleagues and employees. As an anytime coach, you too can tell good stories through your actions, setting an example of positive and productive workplace behavior.

---

### PAF and Listening—Being **P**resent, **A**ware, and **F**ocused

*Listening and being present.* When others are talking, be only in the moment. Allow distracting thoughts (like what they said the last time, what you really want to say back to them, how they might have annoyed you this morning) to just drift away. Return your focus to now. When you do this, you become a more willing and relaxed listener. The speaker will likely sense your suspended judgment and curiosity, thereby increasing the communication bond between you.

*Listening and being aware.* By being only in the moment, you can heighten your awareness of others' voices, vocal tones, facial expressions, and body language so that the words they say stand alone in the present context, untarnished by past assumptions, future projections, or guessing games.

*Listening and being focused.* Choosing to be present and aware allows you to comprehend more fully the broader message the speaker is delivering, thereby enhancing your ability to focus clearly on what matters in the conversation. You will focus on the essence of the conversation.

---

■ ■ ■ ■ ■   **PRACTICE TOOL**
## Working with Employees' Stories

Think of an employee who you believe tells one of the stories we have described (or a different one if none of these apply).

Describe that story.

_____

_____

What new approach might you take to respond to this person's story?

_____

_____

What questions would you ask to help him or her see things differently? Be as specific as possible.

_____

_____

## ■ ■ ■  Listening for Your Own Story

Becoming skilled at listening for common stories and responding appropriately is important. Just as essential is developing your ability to hear and identify your own story or stories. Do you sometimes tell the "I will fix it" story to your manager? Do you sometimes act as if "the sky is falling?" Awareness of your own tendencies will help you understand why you think and say what you do. As described in Chapter 2, The Practice of Observing, self-observation takes time and patience.

---

### ■ ■ ■ ■ ■  PRACTICE TOOL
#### Listening for Your Own Story

Take a moment to think about conversations you have had with your current or former managers.

Can you think of any stories or recurring themes—things you tend to say or think over and over again—that characterize these talks? Describe them.

_____

_____

Consider whether your stories are helpful or not. What do you think?

_____

_____

Describe a new story you would like to tell during conversations with your manager.

_____

_____

---

Extreme listening is an essential practice for Anytime Coaching. You now know that extreme listening requires you to prepare, focus on the person speaking, and listen for "stories." Now that you have learned how to be an extreme listener, what's next? You have to respond to what you have heard. In Chapter 5, The Practice of Responding, you will learn tools and techniques to ensure that your responses are clear and intentional.

■ ■ ■ ■ ■ ■ ■ ■ ■

"It is the province of knowledge to speak, and it is the privilege of wisdom to listen."

—OLIVER WENDELL HOLMES, 19TH CENTURY AMERICAN POET,

PHYSICIAN, AND ESSAYIST

■ ■ ■ ■ ■ ■ ■ ■ ■ ■

### NOTES

1 J. David Creswill, Laura E. Pacilio, Emily K. Lindsay, and Kirk Warren Brown, "Brief Mindfulness Meditation Training Alters Psychological and Neuroendocrine Responses to Social Evaluative Stress," *Psychoneuroendocrinology*, June 2014, volume 44, pp. 1–12.

2 Adam Moore, Thomas Gruber, Jennifer Derose, and Peter Malinowski, "Regular Brief Mindfulness Meditation Practice Improves Electrophysiological Markers of Attentional Control," *Frontiers in Human Neuroscience*, February 10, 2012, p. 1. *http://journal.frontiersin.org/Journal/10.3389/fnhum.2012.00018/abstract*

3 Joshua S. Rubinstein, David E. Meyer, and Jeffrey E. Evans, "Executive Control of Cognitive Processes in Task Switching," *Journal of Experimental Psychology: Human Perceptions and Performance*, 27(4) (2001).

4 Issie Lapowsky, "Don't Multitask: Your Brain Will Thank You," *Inc. Business* online, April 17, 2013. *www.inc.com/magazine/201304/issie-lapowsky/get-more-done-dont*. Also, Travis Bradberry, "The Real Harm in Multitasking," Inc. Business online, January 6, 2015. *www.inc.com/travis-bradberry/the-real-harm-in-multitasking.htmlmultitask.html*.

5 Shafir, Rebecca Z., *The Zen of Listening* (Wheaton, IL: Quest Books, 2000), p. 75.

6 Ibid., p. 238. Dr. James W. Pennebaker is Chair of the Department of Psychology at the University of Austin. His research focuses on language use, health, and social behavior.

7 For another perspective on listening, consider the self-assessment instrument *Personal Listening Style Profile: Understanding Personal Listening Approaches* by Wiley-Inscape Publishing, *www.internalchange.com/personal-listening-profile.asp*.

8 Peter Senge, Art Kleiner, Charlotte Roberts, Richard B. Ross, and Bryan J. Smith, *The Fifth Discipline Fieldbook: Strategies and Tools*

*for Building a Learning Organization* (New York: Doubleday, 1994), p. 244.

9  Ibid., pp. 242–246.

10 Daniel Goleman, Richard Boyatzis, and Annie McKee, *Primal Leadership: Realizing the Power of Emotional Intelligence* (Boston: Harvard Business School Press, 2002), pp. 37–40.

11  Ibid. The four-step model Coaching with Emotional Intelligence is based on Goleman's four emotional intelligence domains and the associated competencies.

12 Willoughby B. Britton, Ben Shahar, Ohad Szepsenwol, and W. Jake Jacobs, "Mindfulness-Based Cognitive Therapy Improves Emotional Reactivity to Social Stress: Results from a Randomized Control Trial." *www.sciencedirect.com/science/article/pii/S0005789411001316*

13 Peter B. Reiner, "Meditation on Demand," *Scientific American*, May 26, 2009. *www.scientificamerican.com/article/meditation-on-demand*

14 Albert Mehrabian, *Silent Messages: Implicit Communication and Emotions and Attitudes* (Belmont, CA: Wadsworth, 1971), pp. 43–44.

15 Dr. Mathew D. Lieberman, *Social: Why Our Brains Are Wired to Connect* (New York: Crown Publishers, 2013), p. 220.

---

## RECOMMENDED READING

Brothers, Chalmers. *Language and the Pursuit of Happiness.* Naples, FL: New Possibilities Press, 2005.

Goleman, Daniel. *Focus: The Hidden Driver of Excellence.* New York: HarperCollins Publishers, 2013.

Krisco, Kim H. *Leadership and the Art of Conversation.* Rocklin, CA: Prima Publishing, 1997.

Loehr, Jim. *The Power of Story.* New York: Free Press, 2007.

Scott, Susan. *Fierce Conversations: Achieving Success at Work and in Life, One Conversation at a Time.* New York: Berkley Books, 2004.

Sharif, Rebecca Z. *The Zen of Listening: Mindful Communication in the Age of Distraction.* Wheaton, IL: Quest Books, 2000.

Stone, Douglas, Bruce Patton, and Sheila Heen. *Difficult Conversations: How to Discuss What Matters Most.* New York: Penguin Books, 1999.

# 5 The Practice of Responding

"Speech is the mirror of the soul; as a man speaks, so is he."

—PUBILIUS SYRUS, 1ST CENTURY BC LATIN WRITER

Once you have mastered extreme listening skills, you are ready to move on to the next practice in the Anytime Coaching model, the practice of responding. When you respond to someone, you deliberately consider what words or questions will move the conversation forward, encourage learning, and create the desired results. As an anytime coach, you will want to learn how to redirect dead-end conversations as well as to expand your repertoire of productive conversation tools.

## Creating Purposeful Conversations

Partner to—and one outcome of—extreme listening skills is good responding skills. The best responses reflect careful consideration of others' statements and an intention to move the conversation forward in a positive direction. Anytime Coaching conversations are like a fluid dance between two partners, listening and responding. Because Anytime Coaching conversations are purposeful and intentional, they require thoughtful and proactive responses as well as the deliberate avoidance of unhelpful comments and questions.

### Your Wise Internal Editor

Anytime coaches have a very active and wise internal editor that helps them respond appropriately in everyday conversation. Do you know an employee who seems to say just about anything that comes to mind—someone who seems to have no internal editor filtering his or her responses? Sometimes people lack the skill to create purposeful conversation that is mindful of the impact of words. They seem not to know how to create—or what to leave out of—effective conversation. Being able to use your wise internal editor allows you to access your higher level executive brain system rather than rely on your more primitive, emotional brain system.

When you deliberately create conversation that is future-focused, outcome-focused, and based more on asking than on telling people what to do, you naturally avoid unproductive, dead-end conversations. Your conversations will not focus on blame, uninformed advice-giving, judgments and labels, gossip, accusations, or complaints.

## Responding to Unproductive, Dead-end Conversations

What should you do when you hear coworkers or employees blaming, gossiping, or judging? Such ways of speaking are like traveling on dead-end streets: You get nowhere. Unchecked, these behaviors can create a negative and suspicious atmosphere in any workplace.

Have you noticed that negative responses stay with you longer than positive comments, especially those from your own manager? According to Judith and Richard Glaser, writing in *Harvard Business Review*:

> *...a critique from a boss, disagreement...can make you forget a month's worth of praise.... Chemistry plays a big role in this phenomenon.... When we feel marginalized or minimized, our bodies produce higher levels of cortisol, a hormone that shuts down the thinking center of our brains and activates conflict aversion and protective behavior. We become more reactive and sensitive. Cortisol functions like a sustained-released tablet—the more we ruminate about our fear, the longer the impact.*[1]

Anytime coaches develop an awareness of negative talk and respond to it in a way that differentiates facts from opinions and speculation and instead focuses on positive, future-oriented, mission-driven possibilities.

| Anytime coaches avoid: | Anytime coaches respond by: |
|---|---|
| Blaming | • Focusing on the facts about what happened and the impact on the work at hand, rather than whom to blame |
| Judgments and labels | • Differentiating facts from opinions<br>• Describing the effects and outcome of actions or decisions |
| Uninformed advice-giving | • Seeking information and collaborating on ideas that drive action forward<br>• Asking the speaker how he or she decided the advice was valid and useful<br>• Collaborating on an action plan |
| Gossip | • Focusing on facts relevant to the work<br>• Differentiating facts from speculation<br>• Talking about how to get the job done |
| Accusations | • Focusing on what the speaker thinks are the facts<br>• Separating opinion and judgment from what really happened and what each party said or did<br>• Coming to a mutual understanding of what both parties want<br>• Creating agreements for future interactions |
| Complaints | • Focusing on clear descriptions of the problem situation and its impact<br>• Collaborating on what can be done to improve a difficult situation<br>• Creating joint processes for solving the problem |

■ ■ ■ ■ ■ ■  **PRINCIPLE**

When anytime coaches hear a dead-end conversation, they know how to respond to prevent negativity from harming the work environment.

Now that you know what kinds of talk to avoid, let's take a close look at ways to respond more intentionally.

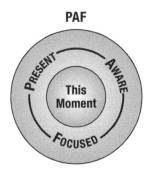

### ▪▪▪ Using PAF to Say the Right Thing, at the Right Time, in the Right Way

You have keenly observed yourself and others, you have asked insightful and open-ended questions, and you have listened with extreme listening. Now it is time to respond. You can enhance your responding skills by being *present*, being *aware*, and being *focused*.

*Being present.* When coaching others, it is easy to be influenced by a flood of racing thoughts about past conversations, about emotions stirred by the speaker's previous actions and behavior, or about concerns for the future and what might go wrong. Being present will help you respond to only what is being discussed at this moment—not the content of past conversations or imagined future conversations. Remember to stay present with just this conversation. Be grounded in the current moment only. Direct your full attention to the topic and to the person—to his or her mood, overall demeanor, vocal tones, and facial expressions as they are occurring right now. Slowing your breathing and directing your eyes toward the speaker will help you stay present.

*Being aware.* Once anchored in the present moment, expand your awareness to notice as much as possible: the speaker's choice of words, speed of speech, facial and hand gestures, body movements, and posture. Be aware of your location—whether people are passing in the hallway, if there are distracting noises, etc. Notice without judgment. With full awareness, you will gain a full picture of what's going on with the other person.

*Being focused.* Having heard and understood what the speaker has said, and being aware of the general mood and environment of the conversation, you can then refine your focus to center on what's important to both you and the speaker. Ask yourself, "What matters most right now?" Is it making a plan? Preserving dignity? Brainstorming new ideas? You can then choose which conversation tool will fit the moment. It might be affirmation, followed by appreciation and reinforcement. Then you might make a request by being clear about what it is you want, the standards for completion, and a timeframe. After a request, you are back to listening again to the other person's response, holding the focus on what matters most in this conversation, while being aware that new topics or new concerns may be introduced.

Remembering to be present, aware, and focused will become more natural as you practice observing with nonjudgmental awareness in day-to-day workplace situations. Making intentional choices about which conversation tool to use will be easier as you take that short moment of quiet observation to select the best response.

## Conversation Tools That Work

Conversation tools are specific ways of using language with deliberate intention. Anytime coaches make sure they use conversation tools that improve relationships and get results. Expanding on language theories that focus on key speech acts,[2] we propose specific conversation tools that can help managers be more intentional with their language.

Anytime coaches effectively use the following conversation tools when responding:

- Invitations
- Acknowledgment
- Affirmation
- Appreciation
- Reinforcement
- Inquiry and advocacy
- Offers
- Commitments
- Proposals
- Clear requests
- Directives
- Reframing
- Declarations.

Each of these conversation tools expands the anytime coach's set of options for responding in positive and productive ways.

### Invitations

Anytime coaches demonstrate that they are open to new ideas by inviting others into conversation. They do this in a variety of ways. They might simply say, "I invite you to tell me your thoughts about this." Or, "I am really curious about how you see our chances of winning the bid." Or, "I want to hear from everyone before we finalize our course of action." In a meeting, an anytime coach might gently encourage the less talkative people to speak up by saying something like, "There are still some people we haven't heard from. Jared, I welcome your thoughts."

## Acknowledgment

Anytime coaches make a point of acknowledging what is said to them. Acknowledgment does not suggest agreement or disagreement; it simply indicates that the other person is being heard. Acknowledgments can be nonverbal, such as a nod or a smile, or they can be statements like "I see" or "OK, I hear you." The first step is to stop what you are doing (checking your email, looking at your phone) and simply look at the other person. Quietly putting other things aside and casting an interested gaze on the person talking to you demonstrates that you are present, aware, and focused. You will find that switching from task completion to fully taking in the words of another has a calming effect on the speaker. Emptying your mind of everything but the speaker's words will help calm you as the listener as well.

Blank-faced silence can confuse people; they want to be sure they are being heard. Acknowledgment in conversation shows that you are listening and (as discussed in Chapter 4, The Practice of Listening) is an important step toward building relationships. Acknowledgment is also an effective way to tame your FRG by focusing on the person rather than jumping to immediate action or problem solving.

## Affirmation

Affirmation means making statements that show you have heard the content of what someone has said. Common affirmation techniques include paraphrasing and summarizing. An anytime coach might say: "It seems you are saying you agree with the new strategy—is that right?" Or "I think your point is that the new budget does not include enough money for your project—is that true?" You can also affirm another person's statements by commenting on that person's thinking or concerns: "It seems you have thought a lot about this." "You have definitely provided a number of reasons for your stance on this." "I can see you are concerned about the direction of the strategy."

Affirmation statements tell the speaker that you were truly listening to understand and are now ready to respond.

## Appreciation

After acknowledging and affirming what the speaker has said, tell him or her what you found valid, important, or unique about the speaker's words, behaviors, or actions. Everyone likes to be appreciated; anytime coaches are always looking for opportunities to voice appreciation. An anytime coach might say something like, "You make a really good point when you talk about customer preferences." "I especially like the recommendations you've made for shifting our marketing approach." "Your statistical analysis uncovered several critical advantages." "I really appreciate your thoughtful approach to the problem." "I think the way you respond to customers is outstanding." Appreciation statements show that you not only are aware of what people are doing well, but you value their contributions.

## Reinforcement

Anytime coaches know that people tend to repeat positive behavior when they are recognized and rewarded for it. When offering appreciation, anytime coaches also reinforce good work by building on their appreciative remarks and connecting what they have observed to the mission and the future. Reinforcement helps strengthen new neural connections, which are critical to create new habits and thought patterns.

Some examples: "I think the way you respond to customers is outstanding. When you hear their complaints, voice your concern, and then pledge to help them solve their problems, you convey this company's dedication to customer satisfaction. I hope you will continue to do that." Or "You handled that situation well, Sarah. You were calm, focused, and you clearly laid out our plans to correct the mistake.

Such clear-headed thinking is going to come in handy when we revise our strategy this year. I would like you to be on our strategy team." Reinforcement lets employees know that their positive contributions are important.

■ ■ ■ ■ ■ ■ **PRINCIPLE**

> Anytime coaches use multiple conversation tools to ensure that their employees feel fully heard. The tools invite ideas, acknowledge employees when they speak, affirm the content of their remarks, appreciate their thinking and work, and reinforce their positive efforts.

### Inquiry and Advocacy

The practice of inquiring is so important to Anytime Coaching that we have devoted an entire chapter to it (Chapter 3). While inquiry is the practice of asking targeted and tactical questions, advocacy refers to the skills used to promote specific ideas. Anytime coaches recognize that advocacy skills are essential to presenting and advancing both facts and opinions.

Clarifying whether you are presenting facts or opinions is a key skill of advocacy, but more important is the ability to balance inquiring and advocating. Too much inquiring may mean you never get your points across, while too much advocating may mean you never learn the facts and opinions behind others' ideas. Anytime coaches know that people are more willing to consider others' ideas when their own have been fully heard and understood. Thus, balancing the two is a skill in and of itself. In *The Fifth Discipline Field Book*, Rick Ross and Charlotte Roberts describe the balancing of inquiry and advocacy as a key skill for anyone in the workplace.[3]

When anytime coaches advocate for their points of view, they use a simple four-step process: labeling what they are about to do; getting agreement; describing their ideas, assessments, and rationale; and asking for feedback.

**Four Steps of Advocacy**

| Step | Example |
|---|---|
| 1. Label what you are going to do. | "I have an approach I would like to share." |
| 2. Get agreement. | "Would you like to hear it?" |
| 3. Describe your idea and rationale. | "A great way to get the results we want is to . . . . This would be the most effective approach because . . . . I base this on my assessment of. . . . Plus, it is simple and cost-effective." |
| 4. Ask for feedback. | "What do you think?" |

A brief advocacy conversation might go like this:

*Louise:* It's been interesting to hear your thoughts, Eduardo, about how to solve the budgeting delays. I think I understand your point of view now. I also have some ideas that I would like to share. Would you like to hear them now? *[Louise labels what she is about to do and seeks agreement.]*

*Eduardo:* Sure, tell me about them.

*Louise:* I think the best way to reduce the time it takes to plan is to publish our budgeting assumptions for our partners a month earlier. I base this on my assessment that they need more time to review the assumptions before we can get their approval. If we get their buy-in earlier, we'll have more time to do our planning. *[She describes her idea and rationale.]* What do you think of that? *[Louise asks for feedback.]*

*Eduardo:* That sounds good. We could do that and also implement my recommendations about the input process, and together those two ideas should give us about six extra weeks to do the planning.

Thanks! *[Feeling fully heard, the employee accepts the new idea and combines it with his own to create a new solution.]*

If managers overpromote their own ideas without balancing advocacy and inquiry, they run the risk of having employees feel overwhelmed and less inclined to present and promote their own thoughts.

## ■ ■ ■ ■ ■ ■ PRINCIPLE

Anytime coaches balance their advocacy and inquiry skills to create an environment where employees know their best thinking is valued and appreciated.

### Offers

Offers are statements of what you are willing to do. Anytime coaches regularly make offers of help to employees. In a one-on-one conversation with an employee, a manager might say, "I am willing to meet with you at 1:00 p.m. the day before your presentation to help you rehearse it." Usually, offers are followed by a question seeking feedback. For example: "Will that be helpful?" While this example is specific and time-bound, offers can also be broader and addressed to a group. These set the stage for a working relationship. For example, a manager might make the following offer: "I will be in my office on Thursday afternoons for unscheduled drop-in meetings." Offers like these show that the speaker wants to engage with others and indicate what the speaker will bring to the relationship.

Offers are wonderful opportunities to create partnerships with employees. But be careful about making them. When someone takes you up on an offer, it becomes a commitment. You must be available and willing to fulfill the commitment; doing otherwise reduces your credibility. If a supervisor plans to offer office hours for drop-in visits on Thursdays, for example, he or she should first ask the group for feedback: "Is it useful to set up a time for impromptu meetings? Would Thursday afternoons be a good time to do this?" If the employees accept the offer, the anytime coach should make a commitment: "OK, I will do this for the next two Thursday afternoons to see how it goes."

## Commitments

Commitments are agreements that something will happen. Managers and employees alike expect commitments to be fulfilled. Once an offer becomes a commitment, the anytime coach simply follows through on the commitment as promised. Should something interfere with your ability to fulfill your commitment, be sure to give notice of the situation as soon as you can, and afterwards, follow up with an explanation and an apology. Consistently fulfilling your commitments will bolster your credibility as an anytime coach.

**Offers and Commitments**

| **Offer:** A statement of what you are willing to do should the listener choose to take you up on the offer. | **Commitment:** When someone accepts an offer, the "offerer" forms an agreement with another person about what will be done. |
|---|---|
| **Examples:** "I can be available on Tuesday afternoons for individual appointments." | **Examples**: "I will schedule one-on-one appointments with each of you on every Tuesday afternoon." |
| "I can show you how I use the software if you think that would help." | "I will meet you at 2:00 so I can show you the basics of the software." |
| "If you'd like, I could introduce you to some people over in the customer care department." | "I will introduce you to Yvette and Juan in customer care on Friday at the office luncheon." |
| "I can invite my manager to come to our next staff meeting if you think that would be helpful." | "I will invite my manager to come to our staff meeting on Monday." |

Anytime coaches make clear commitments to their employees and fulfill them. In return, they seek clear commitments and follow-through from their employees.

*Proposals*

Proposals are statements that suggest a course of action. They are neither directions nor advice. As explored in Chapter 4, The Practice of Listening, anytime coaches know that too much telling can work against sustaining a collaborative relationship with employees. When anytime coaches make proposals, they do so in the spirit of presenting ideas for consideration and discussion. For example: "I propose the team divide into subgroups." "I suggest that we rewrite the analysis, making it more comprehensive." "Let's reconvene next Monday and share our progress." To move the conversation forward, the anytime coach asks for a response to the proposal—and *listens*. The anytime coach then continues to examine the proposal and shares ideas with employees until they reach an agreement that everyone supports. And of course, anytime coaches balance advocacy and inquiry when actively considering others' proposals.

Anytime coaches should remember that a proposal is definitely *not* a directive or an instruction. But be aware that employees accustomed to deferring to people in authority may not immediately understand that a supervisor's proposals are open to discussion. The anytime coach demonstrates that a proposal is different from a directive by encouraging discussion and yielding to persuasion. When anytime coaches hear others' proposals, they acknowledge them and engage in dialogue about them.

*Clear Requests*

Anytime coaches know how to make their requests clear. They are mindful, present, and do not feel overwhelmed (or at cognitive capacity overload) when making a clear request. They know before making a request exactly what they want an employee to do and what outcome they want. They state specifically what should be done, when it should be done, and the parameters or quality of work expected.

As you cultivate a quiet and calm mind, you will find that being clear in your requests becomes easier. Similarly, asking others to stop what they are doing while you make your request will also become easier.

Example: "Vicki, I want you to establish a shared file on drive G with the highest allowable storage capacity by close of business on Friday." An unclear request for the same task might sound like this: "We need a shared file on the network. Can you do that?" This request is not specific enough and might result in disappointment when the employee attempts to fulfill it.

When anytime coaches make clear requests, they are looking for clear responses. They usually expect a commitment from the employee. ("Yes, I will do it.") As noted, commitments are agreements about future action. They encourage accountability and—when fulfilled— build trust and credibility.

Of course, your employee may not agree to your request. You may get a "no," a negotiated "yes," or a negotiated delayed response. "No" is easy to understand, but it doesn't signal the end of the discussion. Ask the employee why he or she is saying no. If "no" is not an acceptable answer, reconsider whether a request was the right tool to use. Perhaps a directive would have been more appropriate.

What is a negotiated "yes"? It means that the employee may say, "I can do this but not that." A negotiated delayed response might sound like this: "I need to check my calendar first, but I will get back to you with an answer by noon." If an employee does not give a clear answer, the anytime coach asks questions to clarify. He or she might say: "Is that a yes?" "Do you need more time to think about this? Will you tell me by noon today if you can do it?" "I'm hearing that you can gather the information, but you cannot finish the forms by

Friday. Is that right?" Clear responses to clear requests ensure that the employee and the coach know who has committed to what.

### Directives

Directives tell people what to do. Although we caution against telling your employees what to do too often, we acknowledge that "telling" is sometimes the right thing to do as a manager. Such times include the following:

- When employees ask for direction: "What do you want me to do next?"
- During discussions about the nature of an employee's job. The supervisor should clearly spell out the duties and responsibilities of the job.
- When directions from your own boss must be passed down without negotiation.
- During performance improvement discussions. The supervisor tells the employee to do something specific (e.g., "You will complete the reports by noon on Friday every week") to better his or her performance.
- During emergency situations, when there's no time for discussion and people must move quickly to resolve a problem. For example: "Call the customer immediately and tell him we are working to resolve the issue." Emergency situations also include those dealing with health, security, or high conflict.

**■ ■ ■ ■ ■ ■ PRINCIPLE**

Anytime coaches make deliberate choices between the conversation tools of offers, commitments, proposals, requests, and directives when responding to employees.

*Reframing*

Reframing is a powerful tool in the practice of responding because it opens new possibilities when someone is stuck. Employees may have ideas or work habits that are unproductive. Sometimes they just cannot seem to let them go, even when there is a gap between their goals and what is actually happening. Anytime coaches use the technique of reframing to open up new possibilities when someone seems stuck. Reframing is the act of suggesting new ways to look at a situation.

As explored in Chapter 4, The Practice of Listening, practices such as relabeling help you consider your thoughts and emotions surrounding an event. Neuroscientists and medical researchers have found that reframing techniques, especially when thinking about a challenging or painful situation, have tremendous positive side effects for well-being. When you reframe, you actually change your thought pattern and can respond differently to the situation, which makes you feel healthier and less stressed.[4]

Here is an example of reframing:

> *Lola:* The people in accounting don't want to cooperate. No matter what I do, they refuse to provide the information I need.

> *Anytime Coach (ATC):* What leads you to believe they don't want to cooperate?

> *Lola:* Well, as I said, they simply refuse to respond to my requests for the monthly updates I need.

> *ATC:* I'd like to ask you a few questions about what's going on. Is that OK?

> *Lola:* Sure, go ahead.

> *ATC:* How do you make your requests?

*Lola:* I call Clarice or leave her a message.

*ATC:* And what does she say?

*Lola:* Clarice says they will get around to doing it, but they never do. And then I leave messages reminding them. It doesn't do any good.

*ATC:* I think there's an opportunity to look at this differently. Can you think of any other explanation for them not giving you the information?

*Lola:* I suppose they could just be swamped with work like the rest of us.

*ATC:* Yes, that could be. What else?

*Lola:* Oh, I don't know. What do you think?

*ATC:* Well, I think you could be right—they might be swamped. I also think there may be something about the way you ask for the information and remind them that may get in the way of your getting what you need.

*Lola:* What do you mean?

*ATC:* Have you explained to them exactly what information we need?

*Lola:* Yes, I tell them we need the monthly updates.

*ATC:* Do you need *all* of the updated figures to get your work done?

*Lola:* No, not all of them, but since they do all the updates at one time, I just ask for the monthly updates.

*ATC:* Could you get by with just parts of the information?

*Lola:* Frankly, yes. I really only need several key figures.

*ATC:* So let's reframe the situation. They think you're asking for the full monthly updates, when you really only need several figures. Do you think that if you restated your request more clearly, they might see that what you want won't create extra work for them—and maybe they could get to it more quickly?

*Lola:* Yes, maybe. If I explain that I really only need the key figures from the overall monthly update, maybe they'd realize it is a small request and do it for me. I will try that.

*ATC:* Do you give them a timeframe when you ask for the information?

*Lola:* I can't remember. What I should be doing is asking for the six figures I need and letting them know I need the information by the last day of the month. That might help them understand what I really need.

*ATC:* Good. Let me know what happens next, will you?

*Lola:* Sure, no problem.

The anytime coach helped Lola, the employee, reframe the situation (from "people from accounting just will not cooperate" to "they might respond better if I make a clearer request"), and she was able to change her perspective of defeat and think of a more efficient and effective way to get results.

Use open-ended questions like these to help an employee reframe a situation:

- Is there another way to look at this?
- What else could be going on here?
- What other possibilities are there?

■ How do you think someone else might see the situation?

■ What if you changed your point of view?

■ What if you saw the problem as solvable?

■ What other facts are there to consider?

■ ■ ■ ■ ■ ■ **PRINCIPLE**

Anytime coaches help their employees get "unstuck" through reframing. They help them examine difficult situations with new perspectives.

### Declarations

Declarations are powerful statements of purpose and intention. An employee who declares, "I am a reliable and trustworthy team member," lets everyone know what kind of person she is and how she intends to interact with others.

Declarations can create new realities. A company that declares, "We protect and invest in the environment," tells the surrounding community that it intends to be environmentally responsible. In turn, the community expects the company to follow through on its declaration and may even partner with it to do so.

Declarations can also help build relationships between anytime coaches and their employees. A manager might declare to her employees, "I value your honesty." Her employees may then envision a future in which they can speak their minds without fearing rejection or reprisals. Such declarations have enormous power—if the "declarer" lives up to the truth of the declaration. It is easy to make declarations, but making them *successful* requires integrity and the ability to act on them. Unfulfilled declarations only erode trust.

Positive declarations can be powerful statements that shape the future. To see how this works, try making a short list of declarations about yourself as a coach. For example: "I am an anytime coach." "I am committed to practicing Anytime Coaching with my employees." "I bring a sense of curiosity to work situations." Writing and repeating declarations like these can restructure your own thinking about what you are doing and what your intentions are. Remember that deliberate creation of new ways of thinking develops new neural connections in the brain that—with repetition—"fire together" and become habit.

What happens when you share these declarations with others? They will develop certain expectations of you, and you will be accountable for your words. Imagine a new supervisor saying to her employees, "Our outstanding service is vital to our customers." Such a declaration creates a particular vision for the team. Its members may begin to think differently about their duties and their customers. They will see themselves as "vital."

---

■ ■ ■ ■ ■ **PRACTICE TOOL**
Creating Positive Declarations

List some positive declarations about:

Your coaching

_____

_____

Your staff or employees

_____

_____

Your role as a manager

_____

_____

Your organization

_____

_____

## Conversation Tools That Trigger Action: The Big Five

Now that we have explored all 14 conversation tools, let's take a closer look at what we call the "Big Five." These are the five conversation tools that trigger action in the workplace—that ensure things get done and lead to incremental performance improvements:

- Offers
- Commitments
- Proposals
- Requests
- Directives.

Anytime coaches expertly use the Big Five conversation tools to ensure that employees clearly understand what actions to take to get the work done. Being clear on the distinctions between the Big Five will ensure that your coaching language triggers actions that lead to ongoing performance improvements.

Here are some examples of how you might use responses that trigger action in the workplace. Perhaps you made an *offer* to review a new employee's work before she submits it to a coworker: "I would be willing to take a look at your report before you pass it on to Sharon." This is simply a statement of willingness—not a proposal, a request, or a directive. Employees see offers as helpful suggestions but may not think that they require action. If the employee hands you her work in response to your offer, you would then make a *commitment*: "I will finish my review of the report by the end of the day." You have promised to do something specific for the employee within a specified timeframe; following through on your commitment will build trust.

If you feel a review would be a good idea but is not necessary, you might say, "I suggest you submit your report to me by Thursday if you would like me to review it by Friday." You've made a *proposal*; the action is suggested but is not required. To maintain credibility with your employees, you cannot hold them accountable for proposals because, by their very nature, they are not mandatory.

If you want an employee to do something specific, you must make a clear *request*. You might say, "Will you email a first draft of the report to me by noon on Thursday?" You might add that you would like the draft by then so you have time to review it. Then you would ask the employee to make a commitment.

If the employee is required to do something, then state a *directive*: "Get a first draft to me by noon on Thursday." Directives tend to shut down conversation and so should be used sparingly.

Anytime coaches do not mislead their employees with offers or proposals when they really want to make a request or direct them to do something specific. Remember that an offer becomes a commitment when an employee takes you up on it, and you should make clear how you plan to fulfill it. Similarly, proposals, requests, and directives trigger action by prompting employees to respond with commitments.

■ ■ ■ ■ ■   **EXERCISE**
## Responding with Offers, Commitments, Proposals, Requests, and Directives

For each work situation listed below, write five possible responses: one phrased as an offer, one as a commitment, one as a proposal, one as a request, and one as a directive.

Example: Reassigning some of an employee's workload to other team members.

a.  As an offer:

"I would be willing to reassign some of your workload to other team members."

_____

b.  As a commitment:

"I will reassign a portion of your work assignments to others on the team."

_____

c.  As a proposal:

"I suggest that we reassign some of your work to others."

_____

d.  As a request:

"By noon Wednesday, would you select a few assignments you think could be reassigned to others?"

_____

e.  As a directive:

"Beginning next Tuesday, you will work only on the top three accounts and you will turn over all other customer files to me."

_____

1.  Coming in early to discuss a current workplace issue with an employee.

a.  As an offer:

_____

b.  As a commitment:

_____

c.  As a proposal:

_____

   d.  As a request:

   _____

   e.  As a directive:

   _____

2. Talking to a colleague about finding a job for one of your employees in another
   department.

   a.  As an offer:

   _____

   b.  As a commitment:

   _____

   c.  As a proposal:

   _____

   d.  As a request:

   _____

   e.  As a directive:

   _____

3. Rescheduling an appointment for later in the week.

   a.  As an offer:

   _____

   b.  As a commitment:

   _____

   c.  As a proposal:

   _____

   d.  As a request:

   _____

   e.  As a directive:

   _____

4. Holding more frequent one-on-one conversations with an employee.

   a.  As an offer:

   _____

   b.  As a commitment:

   _____

c. As a proposal:

_____

d. As a request:

_____

e. As a directive:

_____

## Getting Ready to Respond Intentionally

With at least 14 different conversation tools to choose from, how do you make quick decisions in the moment about which one is best? Time and practice. Practice being more present, aware, and focused during workplace conversations to increase your ability to choose intentionally among the different responses. With time and practice, you will begin making more intentional and effective choices.

Sharon Salzberg, a pioneer in the field of mindfulness, explains how to strengthen the practice of responding with intention:

> *Mindfulness helps us fundamentally know what our intentions are. I always encourage people, before a meeting, or phone call, or encounter with someone, to look within to discover their own intention. What do you most want to see come out of this conversation? Do you want to be seen as right? Do you want to find a resolution? Do you want to thwart their plan? Do you want to help someone? Then you can act accordingly.*[5]

Sometimes it is helpful to reflect on an upcoming conversation and be intentional in planning how to make that conversation successful. You may find the following Conversation Planner helpful.

| Conversation Planner | | |
|---|---|---|
| Conversation: | Other party: | Date: |
| Purpose of Conversation | ☐ Information gathering<br>☐ Clarification | ☐ Problem/solution<br>☐ New assignment<br>☐ Other_____ |
| What do I hope to achieve during this conversation? | | |
| What am I assuming about my conversation partner? | | |
| What listening biases should I avoid? | | |
| What positive possibilities might I realize during this conversation? | | |
| What open-ended questions might I ask? | | |

■ ■ ■ ■ ■   **EXERCISE**

## Identifying Anytime Coaching Conversation Tools

Below are sample statements illustrating each of the 14 conversation tools. Identify which tool is being used. Tools may be used more than once. Check your answers at the end of the chapter.[6]

For reference, here is the list of tools:

- Invitation
- Acknowledgment
- Affirmation
- Appreciation
- Reinforcement

- Inquiry
- Advocacy
- Offer
- Commitment
- Proposal

- Clear request
- Directive
- Reframing
- Declaration

| Sample statement | Which tool is this? |
|---|---|
| 1. My method of tracking milestones for the contract is the one that is most efficient and least costly, and we should begin doing it now. | |
| 2. All right, I can understand your point of view. | |
| 3. Starting next Friday, I will send each of you the updated calendar for the following week. | |
| 4. I believe in open communication between team members. | |
| 5. If you think of the team's lack of direction as an opportunity for creativity, you might be able to think of the next steps to take. | |
| 6. Would you please deliver the proposal to the client's office in a three-ring binder, with a CD included, by 5:00 p.m. on Monday? | |
| 7. Call the technician and tell him we need an immediate response. | |
| 8. I encourage each of you to bring your best thinking to the meeting tomorrow, where we'll begin to discuss next year's strategy. | |
| 9. Your easy-to-understand spreadsheets help the entire team get the information it needs. Your analytical skill can help us in other ways, too. | |
| 10. Your ability to summarize complex data is greatly appreciated. | |
| 11. I hear that you want to reschedule the meeting for later in the month. | |

| | |
|---|---|
| 12. This team is dedicated to the principles of open and honest communication. | |
| 13. I will notify you 24 hours in advance if I must miss one of our appointments. | |
| 14. I welcome your ideas on how to prioritize our team's objectives. | |
| 15. What ideas do you have about reassigning the workload? | |
| 16. Try looking at the situation as a puzzle to solve—a game in which the winner gets to go home early if a solution is found. That might make things seem less dire. What do you think? | |
| 17. I suggest that everyone at the meeting give a brief update on assigned action items. | |
| 18. I can see that you feel passionately about fixing the problem. | |
| 19. What thoughts does the rest of the team have about our recognition and reward methods? | |
| 20. The analysis completely supports my plan to move forward in three distinct phases, so we should adopt this plan. | |
| 21. I would be willing to let you take over this part of the project and be completely accountable for it. | |

## ■ ■ ■ The Payoff for Responding Intentionally

Now that you are familiar with these powerful conversation tools, you have more choices as an anytime coach. You can be intentional in how you choose to respond to your employees. That is, you decide which tools will help your employees feel truly heard and valued. When people feel valued, they are more engaged in their work and do a better job, resulting in stronger overall organizational performance. Responding deliberately with clear intention is an essential practice of Anytime Coaching.

The practices of intentional responding and extreme listening are inextricably woven. Like a pebble tossed in a pond, the positive effects of extreme listening and responding together create ripples throughout the organization. These ripples show up in the constant modeling of nonjudgmental, future-focused coaching conversations. Another ripple effect is the absence of blame and negative judgments, resulting in a no-fear workplace. Finally, employees demonstrate a greater willingness to share ideas and take new action.

### ■ ■ ■ ■ ■ ■  PRINCIPLE

> Anytime coaches approach each conversation with clear intention and purpose. They make the workplace more productive and enjoyable—one conversation at a time.

You are well on your way to becoming an anytime coach when you begin to consciously combine the practices of observing, inquiring, listening, and responding. In the Anytime Coaching model, these four practices surround the piece at the center of the puzzle: improving day-to-day performance. Blending these practices to shape employee performance is the focus of the next chapter.

### NOTES

1   Judith E. Glaser and Richard Glaser, "The Neurochemistry of Positive Conversations," Harvard Business Review Blog, June 2014. *http:// blogs.hbr.org/2014/06/the-neurochemistry-of-positive-conversations*

2   Readers interested in the theory of speech acts may find the following references helpful:

■ J. L. Austin, *Linking Language to Action* (Cambridge: Cambridge University Press, 1985). Austin is a British philosopher of language whose work underlies the theory of speech acts developed later by Oxford-educated American philosopher John Searle and further articulated by Fernando Flores in the business and political arenas.

■ John Searle, *Expression and Meaning* (Cambridge: Cambridge University Press, 1985). Searle is an American professor of philosophy at the University of California-Berkeley, noted for his work defining speech acts.

■ An interesting article summarizing some of Fernando Flores' beliefs appeared in *Fast Company*, Issue 21, December 1998, "The Power of Words," by contributing editor Harriet Rubin. Flores was a cabinet minister in Chile in the 1970s who later studied at the University of California under John Searle and went on to promote an understanding of speech acts in the business and political arenas.

▪ Julio Olalla worked as an attorney in the government of Chilean president Salvador Allende, before spending years in exile in Argentina, and coming to the United States in 1978. He worked with Fernando Flores and later became one of the founders of ontological coaching, creating the Newfield Network in 1991. The concept of speech acts has been taught to thousands of people through the Newfield Network school of ontological coaching. He is the author of *From Knowledge to Wisdom* (Newfield Network, Inc., 2004).

▪ Chalmers Brothers, *Language and the Pursuit of Happiness* (Naples, FL: New Possibilities Press, 2005).

3   Peter Senge, Art Kleiner, Charlotte Roberts, Richard B. Ross, and Brian J. Smith, *The Fifth Discipline: The Art and Practice of the Learning Organization* (New York: Doubleday, 1990), pp. 253–259.

4   Jeffrey M. Schwartz, M.D., and Rebecca Gladding, M.D., *You Are Not Your Brain* (New York: Penguin Group, 2011), pp. 189–190.

5   Sharon Salzberg, cofounder of the Insight Meditation Society in Barre, Massachusetts, has played a crucial role in bringing Asian meditation practices to the West. She is the author of *Real Happiness at Work* (see Recommended Reading). Her remarks here are in response to interview questions posed by the authors.

6   Answers to Identifying Anytime Coaching Conversation Tools (p. 152):

| 1. Advocacy | 8. Invitation | 15. Inquiry |
|---|---|---|
| 2. Acknowledgment | 9. Reinforcement | 16. Reframing |
| 3. Commitment | 10. Appreciation | 17. Proposal |
| 4. Declaration | 11. Affirmation | 18. Affirmation |
| 5. Reframing | 12. Declaration | 19. Inquiry |
| 6. Clear request | 13. Commitment | 20. Advocacy |
| 7. Directive | 14. Invitation | 21. Offer |

## RECOMMENDED READING

Brothers, Chalmers. *Language and the Pursuit of Happiness.* Naples, FL: New Possibilities Press, 2005.

Hanson, Tom, and Birgit Zacher Hanson. *Who Will Do What By When?* Tampa, FL: Power Publications, 2007.

Kegan, Robert and Lisa Lahey. *How the Way We Talk Can Change the Way We Work.* San Franscisco, CA: Jossey-Bass, 2001.

Patterson, Kerry, Joseph Grenny, Ron McMillan, and Al Switzler. *Crucial Conversations: Tools for Talking When Stakes Are High.* New York: McGraw Hill, 2002.

Rath, Tom, and Donald O. Clifton. *How Full Is Your Bucket?* New York: Gallup Press, 2004.

Salzberg, Sharon. *Real Happiness at Work.* New York: Workman Publishing, 2014.

Wilson, Casey. *The Cornerstones of Engaging Leadership.* Vienna, VA: Management Concepts, Inc., 2008.

# 6 Improving Day-to-Day Performance

You have learned the four fundamental Anytime Coaching practices—observing, inquiring, listening, and responding—which create powerful coaching conversations when used together. You have seen how the research in neuroscience validates the effectiveness of coaching behaviors. You have learned the value of being present, aware, and focused for each of the four practices, along with some simple techniques to help you cultivate mindfulness.

Now you have reached the point where these powerful coaching conversations begin to produce positive shifts in employees' workplace performance. These day-to-day performance improvements lead to stronger organizational results over time.

When Anytime Coaching helps employees focus their attention and make choices that lead to performance improvements, learning and change create new patterns of thinking. "We know that it's not hard to change your brain. You just need to put in enough effort to focus your attention in new ways.... When you change your attention you are facilitating 'self-directed neuroplasticity.' You are rewiring your own brain,"[1] writes David Rock, founder of the Neuroleadership Institute. With such self-directed neuroplasticity, people create change, grow, and develop, and the new learning is deeply embedded. This explains why it is essential to their long-term development that employees make small but significant performance improvements on their own.

Anytime Coaching leverages the four practices that enable and support day-to-day performance improvement. At this point, you will see your hard work begin to pay off. You and your employees will begin to reap the rewards of Anytime Coaching.

## Micro Performance Improvements

Anytime Coaching focuses on helping employees achieve small (micro) but significant performance improvements. These improvements are achievable, tangible, and practical. When an employee . . .

- Begins to speak up effectively at staff meetings
- Finishes a report on time after being habitually late
- Catches errors in emails

■ Gradually learns more about a computer application and eventually tries the new software

■ Handles a difficult customer conversation well

. . . he or she has made a micro improvement.

On the surface, these accomplishments may seem small, perhaps inconsequential, but anytime coaches know that it is through these day-to-day achievements that performance continually improves. Eventually, small accomplishments accumulate and lead to larger performance gains, which foster bigger and better workplace results.

Anytime coaches who work with employees to help them create micro improvements are helping them create new, more positive thoughts, solutions, and work habits. Think of your role as a coach who helps reinforce positive habits. Charles Duhigg, in *The Power of Habit: What We Do in Life and Business*, explains the science behind habits:

> *Habits, scientists say, emerge because the brain is constantly looking for ways to save effort. Left to its own devices, the brain will try to make almost any routine into a habit because habits allow our minds to ramp down more often. To deal with uncertainty, the brain spends a lot of effort looking for something—a cue—that offers a hint to which pattern to use.... Over time, this loop—cue, routine, reward—becomes more automatic.[2]*

The four powerful practices of Anytime Coaching help employees make micro changes and hence create new, positive workplace routines. "Habits aren't destiny.... Habits can be ignored, changed or replaced. Understanding how habits work—learning the structure of the habit loop—makes them easier to control. Once you break down a habit into its components, you can fiddle with the gears."[3] Anytime coaches in essence help employees break down change to its component parts.

Mindfulness can also become a positive habit loop for anytime coaches. Holding focus will come more easily to the anytime coach who has cultivated a habit of mindfulness. The repeated practice of letting unhelpful thoughts drift away will create greater strength in maintaining presence, awareness, and focus on an important situation and moving toward positive performance actions.

An employee who begins talking at meetings may also start to speak up more during one-on-one conversations. The once-tardy report writer who now completes work on time can apply that self-management technique to other tasks. Call it momentum or being motivated by success—it works! Anytime coaches actively look for opportunities to encourage these small shifts, recognizing that they are building blocks for bigger results.

Improving day-to-day performance has tremendous benefits for both the coach and employee:

- It helps the employee achieve performance milestones and successes.
- One employee's improved performance, knowledge, and awareness can have a positive effect on the group's overall performance.
- By helping monitor and sustain employee performance, coaches ensure that performance does not decline.
- Focusing on continual learning and growth encourages the brain to create new neural pathways.[4]

Day-to-day performance improvement is at the heart of the Anytime Coaching model.

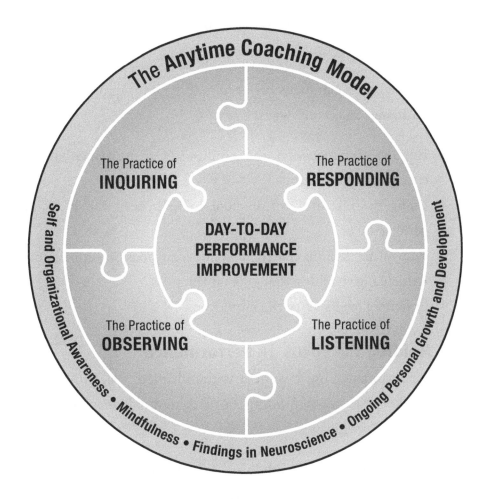

## ▪▪▪ The Goal: Better Results

Observing, inquiring, listening, and responding are specific approaches with particular techniques that guide you through coaching conversations. Improving day-to-day performance is different and more demanding. It calls on your ability to put all the practices together, to synthesize and incorporate them into an effective repertoire that you use in real time. You select which practice tools are most suitable for the employee, the work environment, and the nature of the coaching conversation. When coaching a particular employee, you may need to listen and observe more. Coaching another employee may require you to focus on responding. Ultimately, you choose how you will employ the four practices as you and your employees strive for performance improvement.

The anytime coach can focus his or her efforts on improving day-to-day performance in several ways:

- Holding the focus on the employee's performance during coaching conversations
- Using the circle of results tool to help keep the focus on performance
- Integrating the four coaching practices to focus on performance
- Refocusing coaching that gets off track
- Providing feedback to the employee.

## Holding the Focus on Performance

Because performance improvement is the ultimate goal of Anytime Coaching, keep the idea of *holding the focus* in mind when you begin coaching conversations.

Anytime coaches realize that they—not their employees—are primarily responsible for holding the focus. Employees may not be able to maintain focus on workplace performance for a variety of reasons. Sometimes an employee is distracted, gets mired in details, or needs to catch up on other work. Or there may be an emotional or personal reason why an employee does not want to focus on his or her results (embarrassment about poor performance, for example). It is thus the coach's job to help the employee hold the focus.

The concept of holding the focus is similar to the concept of keeping your ultimate goal in mind. Stephen Covey explains: "To begin with the end in mind means to start with a clear understanding of your destination. It means to know where you are going so that you better understand where you are now and so that steps that you take are always in the right direction."[5]

In Anytime Coaching, you visualize the desired performance or outcome so that you can coach toward that end goal. With this outcome in mind, you can hold the focus in a variety of ways:

- When you begin a coaching conversation, take a moment to make a conscious declaration to yourself that your intent is to hold the focus on performance improvements.
- During coaching conversations, ask yourself, "Am I remembering to hold the focus right now?" Consider writing "hold the focus" on a notecard and keeping it in front of you during coaching meetings.
- Remind employees to hold the focus if they go off on tangents during coaching conversations.

A senior vice president at an international hospitality company shares the value of holding the focus: "My strength as an executive is to stay calm and *hold the focus*. Employees want autonomy and my holding the focus helps them do that."

Here's a story about an anytime coach who finds a way to hold the focus.

### Paul Holds the Focus

Paul, an experienced information technology (IT) manager, has recently moved to a new department in his division. He is now in charge of a new application team, managing six employees. Paul already has a reputation as a manager who uses Anytime Coaching techniques to motivate employees and create an environment of trust; after a few weeks on the new job, he senses that coaching could help improve his new employees' effectiveness.

Paul understands that he needs to hold the focus for his employees during coaching. The focus could be on helping employees change how they answer questions or the tone of voice they use with internal customers. These would be small changes, but they could improve the productivity and visibility of the team.

Paul is able to apply the four coaching practices. He practices extreme listening and responds to employees' concerns with a variety of conversation tools. He uses inquiring effectively, asking employees about changes they can make that would help them work with customers. Paul observes his employees' nonverbal cues when they talk about situations that are frustrating or difficult. He also observes the employees taking calls, noticing the customer-service techniques they use.

Most importantly, Paul quickly recognizes distractions or any resistance from those struggling to change. For example, when employees talk about what other departments are doing, Paul listens briefly, then asks questions to get his employees back on track. Ultimately, the employees recognize that such tangents do not really lead anywhere, and they grow accustomed to Paul holding the focus on their performance. As they succeed in making initial micro changes, they are more motivated to hold the focus themselves in subsequent conversations. They know they can succeed and do not have to rationalize or try to shift responsibility to others.

Holding the focus is also a way to keep your FRG in check, to ensure that you stay focused on micro performance improvements rather than the myriad issues and problems to be addressed in the workplace.

■ ■ ■ ■ ■ ■   **PRINCIPLE**

Hold the focus during coaching to ensure conversations stay centered on improving the employee's workplace performance.

■ ■ ■ ■ ■   **PRACTICE TOOL**

### Holding the Focus with an Employee

Think of an employee you would like to coach to help improve performance. Answer the following questions to help you hold the focus on talking about performance.

What elements of the employee's performance must improve?

_____

_____

What specific steps can the employee take to improve performance?

_____

_____

What can you do to hold the focus on performance during coaching conversations with this person?

_____

_____

## ■ ■ ■  Using The Circle of Results Tool

A practical tool you can use to hold the focus on performance is the circle of results. The circle is an image that will help you organize your thinking about an employee's performance opportunities.

■ ■ ■ ■ ■  **PRACTICE TOOL**
The Circle of Results

The sample circle of results shows examples of performance areas where you may want day-to-day micro improvements.

### Circle of Results Sample

Use the blank circle of results to capture your ideas for a specific employee's micro improvements. You can use it to customize your conversations on performance improvements.

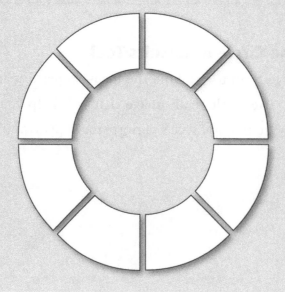

Some anytime coaches fill out the circle tool by themselves in preparation for coaching. Others fill it out together with the employee. The circle is especially useful for employees who are visual learners and respond more favorably to graphically displayed information.[6]

■■■■■■■■■ ■

> "Performance stands out like a ton of diamonds.
> Nonperformance can always be explained away."
>
> —HAROLD GENEEN, AMERICAN BUSINESSMAN,
> FORMER PRESIDENT OF ITT

■ ■ ■ ■ ■ ■ ■ ■ ■ ■ ■

## ■ ■ ■ Integrating the Four Anytime Coaching Practices

Each of the four Anytime Coaching practices of observing, inquiring, listening, and responding creates opportunities for coaching conversations on improving day-to-day performance.

### ■ ■ Observing

As discussed in Chapter 2, The Practice of Observing, anytime coaches pay close attention to the nonverbal communication and feelings that emerge when employees talk about their performance. Performance discussions are significant to employees, so you are likely to see a variety of emotions expressed.

- ■ Does your employee's body language suggest that he or she is more enthusiastic about one aspect of the job than another? Does the employee frown or gesture nervously when you talk about a particular performance measure?

- ■ What tone and pitch does the employee use when talking about job performance? Does the employee's voice indicate frustration or excitement when talking about traveling in the field, for example?

Take notes and share your observations with your employee. The alignment between words, nonverbal cues, and emotions will suggest what the employee thinks of personal accomplishments and challenges.

After observing your employees, take time to observe your own state of mind and do a "head check" (see Chapter 4, The Practice of Listening). Notice whether you have successfully maintained a calm and deliberate demeanor that reflects an inner quiet and confidence or you are instead agitated and distracted by thoughts of risk and uncertainty. Be aware of what you are noticing and engage your favorite methods to return to the more composed, less distractable self you know you can be.

### Inquiring

As explored in Chapter 3, The Practice of Inquiring, open-ended questions are powerful tools to engage employees in performance conversations. Open-ended questions like these can help:

- What aspects of your performance would you like to improve this year?
- What concerns do you have about your performance?
- Where are you getting "stuck"?
- How can I support you in improving your performance?
- What specifically do you think needs to happen to achieve _____?
- What is a very small, daily task that will help you move forward to achieve _____?
- Do you think these performance goals are realistic? Why or why not?
- Are these goals challenging enough for you?

- What other performance improvements would you like to see happen?

- What else is important to you regarding your results? What ideas do you have?

### Listening

Recall the steps outlined in Chapter 4, The Practice of Listening. Before a coaching conversation, have you stepped into the neutral zone and done a head check? Are you prepared to practice extreme listening as your employee talks about goals? What biases do you hold about the employee's performance potential that could impact your listening? Are there any impediments to your listening fully? All these factors could affect your ability to listen.

### Responding

As you prepare to talk with an employee, think about what you learned in Chapter 5, The Practice of Responding. Be intentional in choosing to ask or tell the employee how to get better results. Use a variety of conversation tools to reinforce any performance improvements the employee has already made. Use caution when making offers and commitments, and be clear in your requests for performance changes.

As you integrate the four practices, think about these questions before you begin coaching:

- Do you feel an urge to tell your employee how to do his or her job or how to make micro improvements? Is your FRG taking over?

- What specific, open-ended questions should you ask the employee about making day-to-day performance improvements?

- How can you show appreciation for, support, and encourage an employee's efforts to leave his or her comfort zone? How have you expressed genuine appreciation for previous performance improvements?

■ What responding tools (e.g., invitations, requests, affirmation, acknowledgment) would help you in coaching this employee on performance?

---

**Performance Management vs. Performance Coaching**

Formal performance management is an important set of skills addressed in other books and resources. Our goal in this book is to provide coaching tools and skills that are useful within the context of performance management. We do not, for example, explain how to create a structured performance improvement plan or address how to manage very serious performance problems that could lead to suspension or termination. If you are a new manager, we recommend that you seek help from your manager or your human resources department when you face a difficult performance management situation.

---

## ■ ■ ■ Refocusing the Coaching Conversation

What happens when coaching conversations get side-tracked and move away from discussion of workplace performance? It is all right for coaching conversations to cover a variety of topics, and anytime coaches should be willing to listen throughout. But sometimes these conversations veer far from the topic at hand, which is, in essence, improving the employee's performance.

There is nothing wrong with listening to your employee talk about his or her upcoming trip to Chicago, golf handicap, or child's soccer tournament. We recognize that talking about personal interests helps us get to know our employees, builds greater trust, and strengthens our relationships. But at some point—and you will know from self-observation when you have gotten there—you will have a sense that you need to steer the conversation back to coaching.

When conversations veer off track, anytime coaches use their ability to refocus. Simply tell your employee that you want to return the coaching conversation back to the main topic. (Refocusing is not the same as *reframing*, which is discussed in Chapter 5. Reframing helps a person look at a situation differently.) The anytime coach must make clear the need for the employee to focus on workplace performance improvement.

When refocusing, the anytime coach should make clear that he or she cares about—and wants to focus on—helping the employee make progress. Because coaching conversations should be based on working toward that progress, refocus when a conversation is not productive, even if it is interesting. At the end of a productive coaching session, the conversation should have helped the employee take some step forward. For example, if during a coaching conversation, the employee learns how to complete the budget numbers on time or figures out how to finish a report, the conversation was productive.

■ ■ ■ ■ ■ ■  **PRINCIPLE**

Stay focused to avoid interesting but unproductive coaching conversations that do not move the employee's performance forward.

At the end of a coaching conversation, it is important to take a moment to evaluate the conversation. Was it a nice conversation, one you might have with a colleague or friend over coffee, but not useful? Anytime coaches do not confuse these with real coaching conversations.

■■■■■ **EXERCISE**
### Refocusing and Getting Back on Track

Does one of your employees tend to get off track during coaching conversations? List three topics the employee tends to talk about. What specific things can you say in response to refocus the conversation on performance?

| How the employee gets off track | Ways to refocus the conversation on performance |
|---|---|
| 1. _____ | 1. _____ |
| 2. _____ | 2. _____ |
| 3. _____ | 3. _____ |

The following story illustrates what happens when coaching conversations are interesting but not productive. Ray, a manager, realizes that he must refocus his coaching conversations with his staff.

### ■ ■ Ray Refocuses His Coaching

Ray is the manager of a large compliance team. He recently began using Anytime Coaching techniques instead of relying on the more familiar directive management approach. He now makes time to sit down with staff for coaching conversations over morning coffee. Ray uses more inquiring and open-ended questions than he used to, and employees have noticed that he is friendlier and takes more time to listen. Ray's employees are increasingly comfortable coming into his office and talking about team concerns. He notices that the team's trust, loyalty, and friendship have grown stronger since he began using coaching skills.

Ray's only concern is that the team's work performance has not noticeably improved. A new format for compliance reports continues to create problems for the staff. Ray wants the coaching conversations to help employees get better at filling out these reports.

Ray thinks about how to adjust his own approach toward Anytime Coaching. The coaching meetings are enjoyable and interesting but they are not connected to the team's work outcomes. He realizes that he has never specifically addressed improving performance during coaching conversations.

Ray realizes he needs to *refocus* his coaching. He begins asking employees more questions about how to improve case write-ups and pays closer attention to the difficulties they are having with the report format. He focuses coaching conversations on enhancing reporting, making sure to ask rather than tell the employees how to improve their work. During coaching, Ray and his employees devise strategies each employee can use to improve results. He begins to notice initial performance improvements almost immediately, and the gains become more significant as the employees' confidence rises.

Perhaps Ray was able to think about his conversations with his team calmly because he had cultivated the habit of mindfulness. He has reflected on the positive impact of his coaching and how he can leverage that to achieve enhanced performance. A quiet mind improves the likelihood that day-to-day coaching will be infused with clear intention and focus—focused on the power of the present moment rather than on the past or the future.

## Providing Feedback

"There is no failure. Only feedback."

—ROBERT ALLEN, FINANCIAL AUTHOR

As we continue to focus on improving day-to-day performance, we turn our attention to a technique that is especially effective for Anytime Coaching: providing performance feedback to the employee. Feedback is critical for anytime coaches because it specifically addresses and targets performance—what an employee does well and what he or she could improve.

You can use feedback to help your employees improve day-to-day performance. The Anytime Coaching method of giving feedback incorporates all four coaching practices.

"Feedback is the breakfast of champions."

—KEN BLANCHARD, AUTHOR AND MANAGEMENT EXPERT

### Benefits of Feedback in Coaching

Feedback benefits the coaching process in many ways. It is an effective means of creating learning opportunities out of performance mistakes. It enables the coach and employee to engage in joint problem-solving to correct performance issues. Through feedback, the coach can reinforce positive employee performance, providing external motivation. Finally, feedback can help uncover the root cause of performance problems.

Research suggests that poor or insufficient performance feedback is a cause of 60 percent of deficient employee performance.[7] Feedback can help correct these performance deficiencies.

### Five Essential Principles of Feedback

To give the most effective feedback, anytime coaches should employ the following five principles:

1. *Understand the two types of feedback: positive and developmental.* Positive feedback is a statement of what the employee does well or an acknowledgment of progress. Here are examples of positive feedback:

   - "Tom, I noticed that you turned in the weekly invoice on time to the division director, and I appreciate your timeliness."
   - "You reviewed the budget report and found two errors. That is terrific, Susan. Now our report is accurate."
   - "I received your email about the new schedule. I know you stayed late to send it. I appreciate your commitment."

   If the employee's micro performance improves, anytime coaches remember to give positive feedback in the form of acknowledgment, appreciation, and reinforcement. These responding techniques will help the employee sustain positive performance because they indicate that the coach is fully aware of—and values—good work.

   The second type of feedback is developmental feedback. Using this kind of feedback, a coach can point out opportunities for an employee to make progress, improve, and develop.

   The following are examples of developmental feedback:

   - "Tom, I noticed that the weekly invoice was turned in on Thursday at 9:00 a.m. The division director requests the report by Wednesday at 5:00 p.m. How can we make sure the report gets to the division director on time?"
   - "Susan, I have reviewed the budget reports and found two errors on the spreadsheet. Let's talk about why the errors occurred and how to improve the reports so they do not contain errors."

2. *Balance the feedback.* Anytime coaches balance the amount of positive and developmental feedback they give during coaching conversations. They do not rely solely on either type. Employees need both positive and developmental feedback to improve.

3. *Describe what is observable.* Effective feedback, both positive and developmental, is based on observable facts and information— what you actually see in the employee's work. Do not base your feedback on impressions, opinions, or hearsay. Avoid labeling the employee's work, and stick to the facts. Simple techniques to be more present, aware, and focused may increase your ability to observe more accurately because your attention will be on "what is."

4. *Make it specific.* Generalities and vague feedback do not provide sufficient detail to help the employee understand what he or she is doing well or must improve. Make the feedback as specific as you can. Mention dates, times, people, places, and specific behaviors. The following are examples of specific feedback:

   - *Developmental:* "Susan, I have reviewed the budget reports and found two errors on page 5, column 3, of the spreadsheet. It may be a computational error, or perhaps the numbers were not input correctly."
   - *Positive:* "I saw that you sent me an email at 8:00 p.m. with information on tomorrow's computer repairs. I really appreciate that you went out of your way to make sure I knew when the computers would be fixed."

5. *Make it timely.* Both positive and developmental feedback should be given as quickly as possible. Organizations and managers often rely on annual performance reviews to correct problems and build upon successes, but this is not the best method for boosting performance. Business consultant Ferdinand Fournies writes:

> *Unfortunately, annual feedback is invariably not specific enough, is too late and [is] definitely not frequent enough to improve performance. In fact, it is difficult to find anything you can do once a year that will have a lasting impact upon performance.*[8]

■ ■ ■ ■ ■ ■ **PRINCIPLE**

Remember the five essential principles when giving an employee feedback: know both types of feedback, balance both types, describe what is observable, make it specific, and make it timely.

■ ■ ■ ■ ■ **EXERCISE**
**Receiving Positive Feedback**

Think of positive feedback you recently received. Who gave you the feedback, and how did it make you feel?

_____

_____

Now think about the most significant piece of developmental feedback you have received in your career so far. Who gave it to you? How did this feedback help you learn, grow, and develop?

_____

_____

■ ■ ■ ■ ■  **PRACTICE TOOL**
Giving Feedback

Think of an employee you would like to give feedback during an upcoming coaching conversation.

What type of feedback do you want to give the employee—positive or developmental?

_____

_____

What specifically will you tell the employee?

_____

_____

How did you observe the occurrence you plan to talk about?

_____

_____

When did the event happen? When will you talk with the employee?

_____

_____

What other feedback can you give to balance your main message?

_____

_____

With these feedback essentials in mind, we can consider how giving feedback builds on the four Anytime Coaching practices.

### The Anytime Coaching Method of Giving Feedback

Anytime Coaching feedback incorporates and synthesizes the four practices of observing, inquiring, listening, and responding. For example, anytime coaches:

- Remember to ask important, specific questions and rely on inquiring when giving feedback.
- Use responding techniques to reinforce and sustain performance or help correct performance deficiencies.

- Use feedback to engage employees and strengthen information exchange, relationships, and outcomes.
- Practice extreme listening while giving feedback. Performance improvement conversations are important to both the coach and the employee, and anytime coaches remain focused.

Here's how you can use each Anytime Coaching practice to create useful, effective feedback.

### Observing

When beginning a feedback conversation, anytime coaches share what they have noticed about the employee's work or behavior.

- *Developmental feedback:* "Phyllis, I have noticed that you've participated less in the last three staff meetings. Yesterday, you did not speak at all. Your chair was turned away, and I sensed from your nonverbal communication a lack of interest in being involved. Would you be willing to talk about this with me? I'm concerned because I value your input during staff meetings."
- *Positive feedback:* "Harrison, I noticed that you sounded very enthusiastic about being on the new task force. I wanted to talk with you to make sure you are still excited about it. How can I best support you in making progress and doing good work on the task force project?"

### Inquiring

The anytime coach continues the feedback conversation with questions designed to help the employee explore ways to improve performance.

- *Developmental feedback:* "Susan, I want to ask you some questions about the computation errors on the budget report.

How did you do the calculations? How will you change the computation method you used for the next budget report?"

- *Positive feedback:* "Jane, I noticed that you caught two errors on page 5 of this week's budget report. That is terrific! Did you review the spreadsheet differently? What other ideas do you have to build upon your accuracy in this week's report? Is there something practical and tangible we can do to maintain this great performance?"

### Listening and Responding

The anytime coach demonstrates extreme listening and responding during both developmental and positive feedback conversations. As the employee talks, the coach does not interrupt, and his or her responses directly correspond to what the employee has said. Anytime coaches work hard to stay present, aware, and focused even in the most difficult feedback conversations.

### ■ ■ ■ ■ ■ ■ PRINCIPLE

Use all four Anytime Coaching practices to give effective feedback that helps employees move forward and improves their day-to-day performance.

■ ■ ■ ■ ■ ■ ■ ■ ■ ■

"We often think of feedback as consisting of harsh or difficult messages. Nothing is more untrue."

—John Zenger and Joseph Folkman, leadership authors

■ ■ ■ ■ ■ ■ ■ ■ ■

### ■ ■ Using Feedback to Enhance Employee Performance

Now that you have a solid foundation in observing, inquiring, listening, and responding, you are ready to put all the practices together during coaching and use feedback to enhance your employees' performance.

A brief feedback conversation between an anytime coach and an employee that uses all four Anytime Coaching practices might go like this:

> *Anytime coach (ATC):* Carla, do you have a few minutes to talk about the meeting that just took place with the executive directors? I have feedback that I would like to share with you before your other meetings this afternoon. [*Coach asks for permission to coach and give feedback. Feedback will be timely.*]

> *Carla:* Sure—I have time right now. Will it take more than 10 minutes?

> *ATC:* I don't think so. Thank you for making the time. At the senior directors meeting, I noticed that you seemed very nervous during your presentation. You were talking very quickly during the last half of the presentation to get through all of the Power-Point® slides. I want to find out how you felt during the meeting. What parts of your presentation do you think went well? [*Coach provides specific and timely developmental feedback based on observable information and asks Carla a question.*]

> *Carla:* I felt that the charts analyzing the pros and cons of each option in the plan were well organized. The directors seemed to like the charts. I know my figures were accurate; I spent a great deal of time working on the numbers.

> *ATC:* I agree with you. The charts were really nicely laid out. I hope you will continue to use that clear format in other presentations. What part of the presentation, if any, do you think did not go as well, and why do you think that happened? [*Coach provides specific positive feedback, affirms Carla's assessment of her work, and inquires about trouble spots in preparation for giving developmental feedback.*]

*Carla:* I didn't practice the presentation beforehand and I didn't accurately estimate how much time I would need to go through my slides. It took longer than I had planned, so I started to get nervous. When I get nervous, I talk too fast, my palms begin to sweat, and it is really unpleasant. [*Carla observes her own emotions and nonverbal communication.*]

*ATC:* Getting nervous during presentations happens to a lot of people, including me sometimes. May I make you an offer? I would be happy to meet with you before the next senior directors meeting to hear your presentation in advance. [*Coach acknowledges Carla's feelings, makes an offer.*] Maybe we could talk about how to time presentations. Do any immediate ideas come to mind? [*Coach inquires for ideas.*]

*Carla:* I had not focused on the timing. I have seen you put your watch on the conference table before you present. Maybe that would help me. I have a colleague who uses notecards for important presentations to help her stay on time. Maybe that could work, too. These might be small things, but I will try anything to stop being so nervous. [*Carla demonstrates awareness of an opportunity to improve.*]

*ATC:* I think you are definitely on the right track. Those ideas could really help you. And I would be happy to listen to your presentations ahead of time. [*Coach reinforces performance goals and offers to listen.*]

*Carla:* That would be great. Thanks.

*ATC:* Let me know if you'd like to talk more about ways to feel less nervous during presentations.

*Carla:* I would love to.

The anytime coach uses responding, listening, and inquiring techniques to give developmental feedback in a way that engages Carla. The coach is less a "teller" than he is an "asker"; he does not, for example, tell Carla that she spoke too fast and needs to slow down. Rather, Carla reaches her own understanding of her problem through the Anytime Coaching approach, so she is much more likely to own the challenge and commit to improving. This is an example of self-directed neuroplasticity.

## The Journey of All Four Practices

As on any worthwhile trip, there will be both high and low points as you incorporate the practices of observing, inquiring, listening, and responding in your coaching conversations. You will find opportunities to reflect, learn, and make adjustments. Part of the challenge and excitement of the Anytime Coaching journey is simply being on the path and applying the practices as much as possible.

As you focus on improving day-to-day performance, you will begin to notice tangible progress and growth. Anytime Coaching starts with achievable, realistic steps that build on each other over time, leading to improvements in the workplace.

### NOTES

1  David Rock, *Your Brain at Work* (New York: Harper Business, 2009), p. 209.

2  Charles Duhigg, *The Power of Habit: What We Do In Life and Business* (New York: Random House), pp. 18–19.

3  Ibid., p. 20.

4  Dr. Norman Doidge, in *The Brain that Changes Itself* (New York: Penguin Books, 2006), pp. xix–xx, writes: "The idea that the brain can change its own structure and function through thought and activity is, I believe, the most important alteration in our view of the brain since we first sketched out the basic anatomy and the working component of the neuron."

5  Stephen Covey, *The 7 Habits of Highly Effective People* (New York: Simon and Schuster, 1990), p. 98.

6 The concept of attending to different learning styles when coaching employees is adapted from Howard Gardner's work on multiple intelligences (see Recommended Reading).

7 Louis Csoka, "Closing the Human Performance Gap," *Conference Board, Research Report #1065-94-RR* (New York: Conference Board, 1994).

8 Ferdinand Fournies, *Why Employees Don't Do What They Are Supposed to Do and What to Do About It* (New York: McGraw Hill, 2007), p. 61.

## RECOMMENDED READING

Covey, Stephen R. *The 7 Habits of Highly Effective People.* New York: Simon and Schuster, 1990.

Covey, Stephen R. *The 8th Habit: From Effectiveness to Greatness.* New York: Free Press, 2004.

Csoka, Louis. "Closing the Human Performance Gap," *Conference Board Research Report #1065-94-RR.* New York: Conference Board, 1994.

Fournies, Ferdinand. *Why Employees Don't Do What They Are Supposed to Do and What to Do About It.* New York: McGraw Hill, 2007.

Gardner, Howard. *Frames of Mind: The Theory of Multiple Intelligences.* New York: Basic Books, 1993.

Gardner, Howard. *Intelligence Reframed: Multiple Intelligences for the 21st Century.* New York: Basic Books, 1999.

Goldsmith, Marshall. *What Got You Here Won't Get You There.* New York: Hyperion Books, 2007.

Zenger, John H., and Joseph Folkman. *The Extraordinary Leader: Turning Good Managers into Good Leaders.* New York: McGraw Hill, 2002.

# 7 Your Path to Becoming an Anytime Coach

"To get through the hardest journey we need take only one step at a time, but we must keep on stepping."

—CHINESE PROVERB

Why become an anytime coach? Quite simply, because today's workplace demands it. Every work-related conversation you have with your colleagues, your managers, or your employees is an opportunity to show interest in others' views, clarify assignments, and create a work environment that promotes collegiality, mutual respect, and performance. Technological advances, challenges to work-life balance, the presence of multiple generations in the workplace, and a greater focus on results have all changed the workplace and work itself. These factors also exert pressure on managers and other leaders, influence what they say and how they say it, and necessitate changes in how they manage people.

The four practices of Anytime Coaching give managers ways to interact with others that lead to day-to-day performance improvements. Expert use of the practices also promotes healthy working relationships and creates a positive workplace for everyone.

Anytime coaches practice observing, inquiring, listening, and responding to create powerful conversations. These powerful conversations create small shifts in individual performance that eventually produce organizational results. Leveraging your skills in each of the four practices will help you hold the focus on performance, keep performance conversations on track, and give positive, developmental feedback. To improve day-to-day performance, you must use all the practices with clarity of purpose and have thoughtful, deliberate coaching conversations. It is a big task, but do not be intimidated. Just keep learning and practicing. As you hone your observing, inquiring, listening, and responding skills, you will create a welcoming environment for those you coach to achieve day-to-day performance improvements.

A step along your path in becoming an Anytime Coach is to stay current on what neuroscience tells us about the brain and how that awareness can help you coach more effectively. Continue to discover or create your unique version of everyday mindfulness by experimenting with simple steps that work for you.

## A Way of Interacting Anytime

When you think about Anytime Coaching as something you do daily, you begin to see that it is simply a way of interacting with others at work. Certainly, problems or breakdowns sometimes occur, and the principles of Anytime Coaching definitely apply to issue-centered coaching conversations. But problems are not the only opportunities for coaching. Think of Anytime Coaching as a set of skills and practices you use regularly in daily conversations. Anytime Coaching is truly meant to be used at any time.

You now have a powerful set of skills and practices that you can use in everyday workplace conversations, and you will begin to see performance improvements. Your coaching practices will encourage people to grow and to become more autonomous—to use their best thinking to get the best results.

Anytime Coaching practices require real effort and dedication; in turn, they demonstrate immense respect for your employees and colleagues. By creating an environment free of gratuitous judgment and blame, by focusing on what is said and done rather than on interpretations and judgments, you convey the message, "We all have a stake in getting positive results." Anytime Coaching will help you get the performance your organization is expecting you to deliver *with* and *through* your people.

## Next Steps

So what should you do next to become an anytime coach? How do you begin applying the four key practices? Whether you take most of the actions we suggest or you choose to implement just a few, you will be enhancing your ability to use Anytime Coaching, and you will get the results you are seeking faster.

You will achieve greater success if you have a specific plan for developing and applying the four Anytime Coaching practices. The steps we recommend will help you create an individual plan for becoming an anytime coach

## Learning through Actions

We suggest three types of actions:

- *Actions focused on practicing coaching skills.* We urge you to practice, practice, practice! We provide a model for practicing Anytime Coaching in your work setting.
- *Actions focused on improving your self-awareness and organizational awareness.* We recommend additional ways to learn more about your behavior and thinking as well as your organization's work expectations and culture.
- *Actions focused on building specific skills.* We provide suggestions for actions you can take on your own, actions involving others, and continued reading and writing.

Whatever you choose to do, as long as you do *something* to focus on Anytime Coaching daily, your chances of making these practices work for you will be far greater than if you are simply aware of the practices.

## PRINCIPLE

Anytime coaches continually refine their skills and create specific plans for self-development.

## Practicing the Skills

Whether what you have learned is new to you or is a review of familiar concepts, we suggest that you begin applying your learning to real coaching conversations right away. To add structure to your practicing, choose a single skill or concept you find particularly interesting and concentrate on it for a defined period of time or until you are comfortable applying it. The following is a six-step plan to follow when practicing a new Anytime Coaching skill:

1. *Choose.* Choose a specific skill or concept to focus on. Some examples: observing nonverbal communication, posing open-ended questions, making clear requests, voicing appreciation, and using reinforcement.

2. *Review.* Review the parts of this book that discuss your chosen skill area. Read the text again and discuss it with others. Consider exploring other resources on the same skill or concept.

3. *Observe.* Observe others. Are other managers practicing the skill you have chosen to focus on? Note how others respond to those managers.

4. *Practice.* Practice the skill for a predetermined amount of time. Establish a timeframe that works for you and is appropriate for the skill you have chosen.

5. *Request feedback.* Request specific feedback by asking a trusted colleague or employee to observe you and tell you what you are doing well and what you could improve.

6. *Reflect, connect, and adjust.* Reflect on what you learned from the feedback and connect it to what you already know. Adjust what you have been doing accordingly as you continue practicing the new skill. Repeat steps 4, 5, and 6 as often as you find helpful.

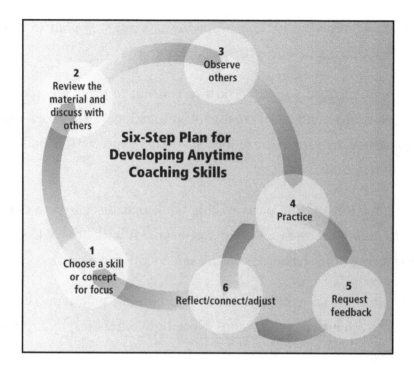

When you are satisfied with your progress, pick another skill area to practice.

## Improving Awareness of Self and Organization

A great place to begin is to find ways to improve both your self-awareness and your organizational awareness.

### Self-Awareness

In Chapter 1, It All Begins With You, you completed informal self-assessments designed to help you understand what thoughts you carry with you about work, what it means to be a manager, how you view your skills and preferences, and your organizational environment. To carry this exploration further, consider the following suggestions:

*Take additional formal self-assessments.* Consider learning more about yourself by completing additional formal self-assessments,[1] such as the widely used Myers-Briggs Type Indicator®, the DiSC®, and the FIRO-B®. You will gain additional knowledge about your tendencies and preferences as well as insight into how your behavior may affect others. At the same time, you will learn about others' preferences and general behavior patterns. You will begin to see Anytime Coaching practices with eyes newly opened by greater self-awareness.

A fundamental piece of wisdom often gained from taking this step is the realization that others do not see the world as you do and therefore may respond to it (and you!) quite differently. But differently does not mean wrongly. Carrying this wisdom into your coaching practices enables you to be less judgmental when observing others and to enter into Anytime Coaching conversations with a spirit of curiosity and learning.

*Continue to check your internal dialogue.* We humans continuously form thoughts as we engage in our daily activities. Once formed, those thoughts shape how we see the world around us. To begin coaching conversations in the best frame of mind, take time to think about your thinking. As explored through the lens of neuroscience and mindfulness, you are creating new neural pathways and connections or, as psychologist Donald Hebb famously said, "neurons that fire together wire together."[2] You won't be aware of the new neural pathways, but they will be taking shape as you practice Anytime Coaching.

Always be aware of thoughts that predispose you to see things and people a certain way. If you routinely think of a particular person as lazy and lacking initiative, for example, it will be more difficult for you to notice when he is energetic and proactive. If you routinely think, "Things around here never change," you will have a harder time implementing incremental change in your part of the workplace.

So check out your internal dialogue and your "story." Ask yourself questions like these:

- What am I already thinking that gets in the way of seeing things in a new light?
- What reframing questions could I ask myself?
- What are my assumptions about the situation?
- What new assumptions may be helpful?

Notice how your internal landscape contributes to your view of the external landscape. Once you develop a regular mindfulness practice, checking your internal dialogue becomes both routine and easier.

*Check your intentions.* While thinking about your thinking, consider what you really want from your Anytime Coaching conversations. Figure out what results are truly important. Decide what impact you want your words to have. Ask yourself questions that help you refine your intentions. Here are some to get you started:

- What outcome do I want from this conversation?
- What atmosphere do I want to create for the team?
- What declarations can I make to create the workplace and atmosphere I want?
- What can I say to help a person share his or her ideas?
- What can I say to let an employee know I truly hear his or her concerns and feelings?

*Develop a habit of mindful meditation.* In addition to building in "mindful minutes" throughout your day (as described in Chapter 2, The Practicing of Observing), consider taking a formal meditation class or yoga. Make mindfulness a priority for your ongoing development. The resulting ability to quiet the mind and be present, aware, and focused will greatly and positively impact your coaching.

*Write it down.* Writing out goals and intentions helps make them more real to you and thus increases the likelihood that you will achieve them. In addition, a person who writes down intended actions is more likely to follow through by creating new positive habit loops.[3] Writing down your goals is so effective because "it forces momentary awareness of what you are thinking or feeling. What's more... writing down a few words helps in later recalling what you were thinking at the moment."[4]

Some people find it helpful to keep a journal as they apply new learning. If you are one of those people, choose a quiet time during the day to jot down what is concerning you, what is getting in your way, or what attitudes and approaches might be nonproductive. To counteract worries and break down mental barriers, write short, positive statements about what kind of environment you want to create at work and how you are going to do it; how you view your employees and how you could improve your interactions with each of them; and what you want the outcomes of coaching conversations to be, in both general and specific conversations.

Skeptical about journaling? Set aside notions of fancy notebooks, eloquent paragraphs, and high-minded musings. A learning journal can be whatever you want it to be. Whether you use paper, a smartphone, or the latest technology available, think about recording what you intend to do, what you actually end up doing, and your reflections on what happened and what you learned. As your inquiring skills grow, write questions to guide your learning journey and then respond to them in your journal. Writing is a distinctly different mental activity from just thinking about Anytime Coaching practices. Writing adds an element of structure to your learning and reinforces it.

Even if you think that "writing stuff down" is not for you, or you think you just do not have the time, give it a try anyway—you might change your mind when you see real results.

### Organizational Awareness

Part of becoming a successful anytime coach is getting to know your organization better by looking around your workplace with a fresh perspective. Here are some ideas to deepen your understanding of your organization.

*Vision, mission, goals.* Knowing what your organization expects of you and your people is the critical first step. Be sure you know the vision, mission, and goals of the larger organization and, more importantly, how your, your boss', and your employees' objectives fit in. Be familiar with any strategic plans and your role in them. Knowing these fundamentals becomes even more important as the pace of change in the workplace accelerates. Creating connections in coaching conversations to larger organizational goals helps your employees see why what they are doing is important.

*Organizational values.* Find out if your organization has a list of stated values. If so, think about whether you have heard your own manager or your manager's manager refer to these values or act in accordance with them. What conclusions can you draw from the way organizational values are referred to or modeled by upper-level management?

Once you are familiar with your organization's values, you can refer to them during coaching conversations to create linkages to your employees' work. At the beginning of a performance year, for example, you can incorporate a discussion of these values in individual or team planning discussions.

*The leaders around you.* Now that you are aware of the Anytime Coaching approach, you are in a stronger position to observe the leaders around you. Are they tellers or askers? A blend of both? If supervisors and managers in your organization are mainly tellers, then they, your colleagues, or your employees may think that the question-asking and extreme-listening practices of Anytime Coaching are unusual. Asking questions might even be perceived as a sign of weakness. One way to reduce others' possible discomfort is to label and explain your new Anytime Coaching behaviors. For example, when you want to ask a series of open-ended questions, you might say something like this: "I think I hear what you are saying. I want to ask you some questions to make sure I understand the situation, and then I will respond with some of my ideas. Is that OK?"

In a workplace full of supervisors and managers who are mainly questioners, the environment might feel more like a daily inquisition. There may be too many "why" questions (implying blame), too many closed-ended questions (implying that little explanation is wanted or needed), and too little follow-up and discussion of the answers (implying that the answers are not respected). In such an environment, people may have a hard time accepting and understanding the questions posed by an anytime coach because they are on guard against an interrogation.

If this is the case, you will have to show through open-ended questions, paraphrasing, thoughtful responses, and extreme listening to employee answers that you are not simply conducting an interrogation. Instead, you must demonstrate that you are helping employees change and work toward desired results. As you question, listen, and respond in accordance with the Anytime Coaching model, it will become apparent that you are respectfully seeking points of view, opinions, and potential solutions. If other supervisors and managers in your environment do the same, it will be easier for employees to adjust to and appreciate the changes stemming from Anytime Coaching.

When you think about the managers in your organization, you may realize that some are already masterful coaches, and you are just now really noticing what they are doing. You can learn a lot from these role models.

*Employee surveys.* Another thing you can to do to understand your work environment better is ask your manager if any recent cultural or climate studies with employees have been completed and if he or she would share the results. Some organizations conduct 360-degree assessments[5] for individual managers and then create a composite report of overall findings, keeping individual results confidential but making organizational trends available to managers. From such assessments, you can learn how the organization's employees view managerial behavior in general and what they want from their workplace. Knowing more about employees' perspectives gives you a bigger picture. What you learn may give you even more insight into how your coaching behaviors will be viewed. You may also learn about specific areas in which employees seek changes, and you can target your Anytime Coaching accordingly.

*Looking from the outside in.* Try looking at your organization as an outsider. Try to discern trends, approaches, and underlying assumptions. Consider how these affect you and how you work. For example, is there an atmosphere of fear or blame? Or an atmosphere of sharing and risk-taking? Does everyone watch the clock? Or do most employees go the extra mile? These types of questions may help you view your Anytime Coaching skills in a broader context and apply those skills more strategically.

■ ■ ■ ■ ■ **EXERCISE**
## Looking at Your Workplace from the Outside In

Below are some common workplace assumptions placed on continuums. Place
a checkmark somewhere along each continuum to indicate how you view your
organizational climate. When you are done, consider how each of these factors
may affect your employees and how you coach them.

●━━━━━━━━━━━━━━━━━━━━━━━━━━●

We work the required hours
and no more.

We pitch in during crunch times
to get the job done.

●━━━━━━━━━━━━━━━━━━━━━━━━━━●

Taking risks is severely punished.

We are rewarded for taking risks.

●━━━━━━━━━━━━━━━━━━━━━━━━━━●

No one cares what I think.

I am frequently asked for my
opinion or input.

●━━━━━━━━━━━━━━━━━━━━━━━━━━●

Getting the work done is what matters
around here.

People really matter around here.

●━━━━━━━━━━━━━━━━━━━━━━━━━━●

My work is inconsequential.

My work is vital to the organization.

●━━━━━━━━━━━━━━━━━━━━━━━━━━●

We keep our heads down and
attract no attention.

We make our ideas known
and feel free to speak up.

●━━━━━━━━━━━━━━━━━━━━━━━━━━●

Decisions are made, and we must
accept them.

We have input on decisions and can
discuss their pros and cons.

●━━━━━━━━━━━━━━━━━━━━━━━━━━●

Things never change around here.

We are making positive progress
toward important changes.

We blame management for all the problems.

We know we have a hand in creating or sustaining the problems around here.

Management has to fix everything.

We actively work to fix problems within our control.

What general statements can you make about your work climate?

_____

_____

How does the general work climate affect how you coach your employees?

_____

_____

If your assessment of your work environment indicates that significant and difficult challenges lie ahead, be aware that you may have limited ability to resolve problems—and that change may take time. Even so, employees will likely notice and appreciate your individual efforts and use of Anytime Coaching practices. Even in a difficult environment, continue to be fully present in each conversation, continue to observe without prejudgment, continue to exhibit extreme listening, and continue to respond and question with clear intentions. Why? Because Anytime Coaching conversations will move things forward. The resulting incremental changes can transform how employees view you and their workplace, as well as the results they achieve.

### Building Skills While Involving Others

While some people prefer learning on their own, many find that working with others is helpful. When people agree to share their learning journeys, they can hold each other accountable and offer each other feedback. The following are some ways to involve others in your path to becoming an anytime coach.

*Get a learning partner.* Invite a fellow manager interested in practicing Anytime Coaching skills to be a learning partner. Make a plan for several months of learning activities.

**Sample Learning Plan with a Partner**

| What we will do | How we will do it | When we will do it |
| --- | --- | --- |
| Practice coaching each other. | We will ask each other for coaching. | At lunch every day for ten minutes |
| Find an online course about managers as coaches. | We will take the course independently and discuss it at break times or lunch. | Within 90 days |
| Find another manager or managers who use Anytime Coaching skills. | We will observe the behaviors around us and share our thoughts on what skills we see others practicing. | Within 30 days |
| Ask managers we think are good anytime coaches to observe us coaching and give us feedback. | We will have the managers observe our lunchtime coaching practice or invite them to listen in on a real coaching conversation. | Within 60 days |
| Find a resource on coaching. | We will share the resource with each other and summarize key points. | Within 90 days |

*Consider involving your manager.* Tell your manager about your decision to develop Anytime Coaching skills. Explain in your own words what you will be doing and ask for his or her support. If you think your manager can give you good feedback on your Anytime Coaching skills, invite him or her to observe you and share those observations. Engage in frequent dialogue with your manager about the changes in your behavior as an anytime coach and how these changes are affecting your employees and their performance.

*Take classes.* Find classes focused on workplace coaching, listening, and related topics. When in class, be sure to talk with others about what is working well for them, whether there are good role models in their workplace, and which relevant books they have read. Consider taking courses with your learning partner(s); discuss what you have learned, practice new skills with each other, and give each other feedback. In addition to classroom-based courses, look for online learning opportunities.

*Get feedback*. Let others around you know that you are learning coaching skills. Ask people you trust and whose opinions you value to give you feedback. When asking for feedback, ask open-ended questions to encourage more detailed responses. Explain what you want feedback about, when you want it, and how you would like it delivered. Here is a sample dialogue that illustrates asking for feedback from a peer.

*Anytime Coach (ATC):* Jordan, could I ask you a favor?

*Jordan:* Sure, what is it?

*ATC:* I've been reading a lot lately about how to be a more effective manager. One of the things I am working on is asking better questions—questions that really help other people think and not make them feel as if I'm just interrogating them.

*Jordan:* I think I see what you mean. What can I do?

*ATC:* I am going to try asking better questions at the upcoming staff meetings, but I might not get the hang of it right off the bat. Would you be willing to listen to the questions I ask and tell me what you think afterward? I would like you to tell me if my questions were open-ended and if they successfully uncovered some new thinking and encouraged people to talk. That way, I can get an idea of how I am doing.

*Jordan:* I could do that. We have a staff meeting coming up tomorrow, don't we?

*ATC:* Yes. Can we make a point of talking afterward?

*Jordan:* Sure thing. No problem.

Jordan will have to focus intently on his listening and observing skills to give useful feedback, and the anytime coach will learn from another person's point of view. You can request feedback from a variety of people in your workplace to get multiple perspectives.

*Find Anytime Coaching role models.* When you observe other managers in your workplace, you may discover a few who are skilled in Anytime Coaching practices. Engage them in dialogue. Tell them what you have noticed. Share your admiration and your interest in developing your own skills. Once you develop rapport, consider proposing an ongoing series of conversations to continue your learning. It is possible that you will find a fellow manager who is willing to act as a mentor as you work toward becoming an anytime coach.

*Consider getting a coach.* Consider engaging a professional coach to help you become an anytime coach. Your organization might already have a list of qualified coaches who work with your colleagues. If not, you can independently hire a coach trained to help organizational leaders develop coaching skills. The International Coach Federation maintains a publicly accessible list of certified coaches at *www.coach-federation.org;* you can search the list by geographic area.

## Your Unique Path

You undoubtedly already know and employ many of the practices of Anytime Coaching. Adopting new practices requires change, and sustaining change requires a variety of support mechanisms. Use the Anytime Coaching principles and concepts to help and support you as you create your unique path to becoming an anytime coach.

Whether you work toward becoming an anytime coach mostly on your own or with the help of others, whether you read a lot or just a little more about coaching, neuroscience, and mindfulness, Anytime Coaching begins with *you*—anywhere, anytime.

### NOTES

1   For more information on the Myers-Briggs Type Indicator® and the FIRO-B®, visit the Consulting Psychologists Press website, *www.CPM.com*. For the DiSC® profile, visit *www.everythingdisc.com*.

2   Donald Hebb, *The Organization of Behavior* (New York: Wiley and Sons, 1948).

3   Charles Duhigg, *The Power of Habit: What We Do In Life and Business* (New York: Random House, 2014), pp. 18–19.

4   Ibid., p. 279.

5   A 360-degree assessment is based on feedback from an employee's direct reports, peers, team members, and supervisors. Today, most are completed online, and reports provide summaries that preserve the anonymity of the responders.

### RECOMMENDED READING

Braham, Barbara, and Chris Wahl. *Be Your Own Coach.* Menlo Park: Crisp Learning, 2000.

Harp, David. *Mindfulness to Go: How to Meditate While You're On the Move.* Oakland, CA: New Harbinger Publications, 2011.

Kabat-Zinn, John. *Mindfulness for Beginners.* Boulder, CO: Sounds True, Inc., 2013.

Marturano, Janice. *Finding the Space to Lead: A Practical Guide to Mindful Leadership.* New York, NY: Bloomsbury Press, 2014. Marturano, former vice president and general counsel for General Mills Corporation, initiated the company's first program in mindful leadership in the mid-2000s and founded the Institute for Mindful Leadership in 2008.

Neumann, Rachel. *Not Quite Nirvana: A Skeptic's Journey to Mindfulness.* Berkeley, CA: Paralax Press, 2012.

Silsbee, Douglas K. *The Mindful Coach.* San Francisco: Jossey-Bass, 2010. While written for the audience of professional coaches, the seven roles also apply to leaders in the workplace who want to coach their employees to be more effective at and more satisfied in the work they do.

## ADDITIONAL RESOURCES FOR YOUR PATH TO BECOMING AN ANYTIME COACH

To continue learning more about how findings in neuroscience are changing the way we work and manage work, consider the following information resources:

- The Academy of Brain-based Leadership has a brain-science orientation and offers a brain-based assessment for leaders. *www.academy-bbl.com.*
- *https://www.neuroleadership.com.* The NeuroLeadership Institute, led by David Rock, focuses on the application of neuroscience findings in the fields of leadership, management, and coaching.
- The annual Neuroleadership Summit presents cutting-edge findings in organizational effectiveness, leadership development, and human performance improvement based on the latest findings in neuroscience.
- "The Neuroscience of Effective Leadership," *Fast Company*, January 23, 2014.
- "The Neuroscience of Leadership: Practical Applications," a 2014 white paper by Kimberly Schaufenbuel, program director of University of North Carolina Executive Development.
- "How Could Neuroscience Change the Way We Manage Change," by Dr. Erica Garms, fourth of a four-part series on what the Human Capital Community of Practice can learn from neuroscience, February 6, 2013. Published by the Association for Talent Development.

To continue learning more about how mindfulness is becoming "mainstream" in the business world, consider the following:

- Congressman Tim Ryan's (D-Ohio) *A Mindful Nation, How a Simple Practice Can Help Us Reduce Stress, Improve Performance, and Recapture the American Spirit* (Carlsbad, CA: Hay House, Inc., 2012).
- The Foundation for a Mindful Society publishes a magazine called *Mindful*, featuring articles highlighting people and developments in how mindfulness is evolving in settings like the military, education, politics, neuroscience, medicine, healthcare, business, prisons, at-risk youth, and psychotherapy.
- "Mindfulness in the Age of Complexity," interview with Ellen Langer in *Harvard Business Review*, March 2014. Dr. Langer is a social psychologist and professor at Harvard University who has written more than 200 research articles for general and academic readers on mindfulness.
- An example of mindfulness workshops offered at the university level is the week-long "Lead Mindfully Workshop—Mindfulness Practice for Execs" at the University of Virginia Darden School of Business. Many other universities currently offer or are launching similar classes in mindfulness in the business disciplines.

# Principles of Anytime Coaching

Anytime coaches notice their employees' positive qualities and look for positive possibilities in them.

===============

Anytime coaches pay close attention to all aspects of communication, including verbal (words), voice (tone), and visual (nonverbal).

===============

Anytime coaches observe the congruence or disparity in verbal and nonverbal communication with their employees.

===============

To resist the temptation to tell your employees what to do during coaching, you must tame your fast results gene (FRG).

===============

Anytime coaches remember that recent findings in neuroscience support coaching practices that help others "rewire" their brains for new actions and results.

===============

Anytime coaches strive to be more present, focused, and aware when interacting with others in order to get better results.

―――――――

Anytime coaches recognize that questions are the doorway to meaningful conversations with employees.

―――――――

Anytime coaches match the purposes and types of question to ensure their questions elicit the best answers.

―――――――

Anytime coaches believe they do not have time *not* to ask good questions and engage in powerful conversations.

―――――――

Extreme listening is listening with complete attention to what the speaker is saying and intends.

―――――――

Anytime coaches are aware of and manage their listening biases to achieve extreme listening.

―――――――

Extreme listeners exhibit nonjudgmental curiosity during work conversations.

―――――――

Anytime coaches balance telling and asking behaviors while exhibiting extreme listening.

―――――――

Anytime coaches believe the best work often results from a collaborative process and listen with this in mind.

―――――――

Anytime coaches listen for opportunities to give people a chance to grow.

―――――――

Anytime coaches listen for emotion—others' and their own—and step into a neutral zone, ready to hear what the other person is saying.

=================

Through extreme listening, anytime coaches recognize common employee "stories" and guide employees to new ways of thinking, speaking, and acting.

=================

When anytime coaches hear a dead-end conversation, they know how to respond to prevent negativity from harming the work environment.

=================

Anytime coaches use multiple conversation tools to ensure that their employees feel fully heard. The tools invite ideas, acknowledge employees when they speak, affirm the content of their remarks, appreciate their thinking and work, and reinforce their positive efforts.

=================

Anytime coaches balance their advocacy and inquiry skills to create an environment where employees know their best thinking is valued and appreciated.

=================

Anytime coaches make deliberate choices between the conversation tools of offers, commitments, proposals, requests, and directives when responding to employees.

=================

Anytime coaches help their employees get "unstuck" through reframing. They help them examine difficult situations with new perspectives.

=================

Anytime coaches approach each conversation with clear intention and purpose. They make the workplace more productive and enjoyable—one conversation at a time.

═══════════

Hold the focus during coaching to ensure conversations stay centered on improving the employee's workplace performance.

═══════════

Stay focused to avoid interesting but unproductive coaching conversations that do not move the employee's performance forward.

═══════════

Remember the five essential principles when giving an employee feedback: know both types of feedback, balance both types, describe what is observable, make it specific, and make it timely.

═══════════

Use all four Anytime Coaching practices to give effective feedback that helps employees move forward and improves their day-to-day performance.

═══════════

Anytime coaches continually refine their skills and create specific plans for self-development.

═══════════

# Index